Who Will Raise the Children?

Who Will Raise the Children?

New Options for Fathers (and Mothers)

JAMES A. LEVINE

J. B. LIPPINCOTT COMPANY
Philadelphia & New York

Excerpts from "Lesson from Sweden: The Emancipation of Man" by Olof Palme are taken from *The Future of the Family,* © 1972 by Louise Kapp Howe. Reprinted by permission of Simon & Schuster, Inc.

Excerpts from "Lessons from a Primate: Males Can Raise Babies" by Gary Mitchell, William K. Redican, and Jody Gomber, © 1974 Ziff-Davis Publishing Co., are reprinted by permission of Psychology Today Magazine.

Excerpts from "Legislative Reform of Child Custody Adjudication" by Phoebe C. Ellsworth and Robert J. Levy, which appeared on pages 167–223 of Volume 4:2 of the *Law and Society Review,* © 1969 the Law and Society Association, are reprinted by permission of the Law and Society Association.

Excerpts from *Baby and Child Care* by Benjamin Spock, M.D., © 1945, 1946, 1957, 1968, 1976 by Benjamin Spock, M.D., and reprinted by permission of Simon & Schuster, Inc., Pocket Books Division.

U.S. Library of Congress Cataloging in Publication Data

Levine, James A
    Who will raise the children?

    Includes bibliographical references.
    1. Fathers.   2. Father and child.
3.   Single-parent family.   I.   Title.
HQ756.L47   301.42'7   76–18743
ISBN–0–397–01120–2

For Joan, Jessica, and Joshua
And for my father,
Alvin L. Levine

CONTENTS

ACKNOWLEDGMENTS

This book could not have been written without the help of many people.

First of all, I wish to thank all those who shared with me their time, homes, a glimpse of their lives. While I quote a few of them directly in the text, in most cases I have preserved their anonymity by changing names and places. For permission to use their real names and the names of their children, I am grateful to the following people: Ken Finlayson, Roger Gatke, Kurt and Courtney Gordon, Linda and Graham Gordon, Jim Green, Everett Hafner, Raymond Jurasin, Tony Piazza, Peter and Vicki Prince, and Al and Ann Woodhull. Many people who spent long hours with me will not find their words quoted or their lives described on the printed page; I want them to know, however, that every minute with them helped give this book perspective, focus, and, I hope, depth.

It was while working at Circle Preschool, thanks to Celeste Myers, that I first began developing some of the ideas—and perhaps the consciousness—for approaching this topic. The Ford Foundation provided the fellowship that allowed me to devote full time to researching and writing this book. From beginning to end it was nurtured along by Susan Berresford, Robert Fein, Mary Rowe, and Joan Levine; all read outlines and various drafts of my manuscript, and none failed to come to the rescue when it seemed I had lost my way and would never finish. I am also grateful to the incisive comments and support of several others who reviewed the manuscript, in whole or in part: Carolyn Shaw Bell, Diana Dubroff, Doris Jonas Freed, Henry Goldman, Mary C. Howell, Milt Kotelchuck, Peggy Daly Pizzo, and John Kinney, my editor at Lippincott.

Among the many friends and colleagues all over the country who helped me locate the families I interviewed, I would especially like to thank Emily Brown, Ann Ellwood, Gunhild Hagestad, Jack Hailey, Barni Olmsted, Hope Marindin, June

Sale, Judy Samuels, Judith Schaeffer, Alice Spears, Joyce Sullivan, and Marlene Weinstein.

Experts in several of the fields I ventured into—family law, psychology, adoption, economics, and early education—gave generously of their time and knowledge and helped me track down relevant information. They include David and Linda Bailey, Sandra Lipsitz Bem, Lenore K. Campbell, John DeFrain, Diana Dubroff, Brenda Broz Eddy, Marc Feigen Fasteau, David Gangsei, Paul Glick, Jim Harrison, Jo Hartley, Mary Janney, Betty Kulleseid, Robert LaCrosse, Michael Lamb, Robert LeClair, Joyce Lynn, Virginia Martin, Dorothy Murphy, Arlene Nash, Edward Neira, Liz Prescott, George Purvin, Robert Rapoport, William Redican, John Ross, Richard Ruopp, Lee Salk, Peter Sauer, Sylvia Donoghue Smith, Barbara Sprung, Linda Stebbens, D. Alwyn Stivers, Myra Stroeber, Joyce Sullivan, Rena Uviller, Kathy Weingarten, Beatrice Whiting, and George Williams. Gwen Davis of the Child Welfare League of America always kept me in mind; every researcher should have a librarian like her as an ally!

I am grateful to Lillian Rubin for sharing with me her system for keeping track of "qualitative data," and for admonishing me to "Write fast!" Would that I had been better able to follow her advice!

Michele Andavall typed and kept track of most of my correspondence at the beginning of this project; Ethel Goldman hunted down obscure articles and provided vegetable soup to boot; Ed Goldman offered numerous legal articles and hot showers. Ginny Bradberry patiently kept track of all the changes in the manuscript and brought it to its typed completion.

My daughter, Jessica, who accompanied me on many interviews and who often watched me pound away at the typewriter, lent this work a delightful perspective. When people asked her what her daddy did she was always quick to explain, "He's a typist." Now that this book is completed, she asks if we can do more interviews for a book she wants to write about children taking care of men!

It hardly seems possible to offer sufficient thanks to my wife, Joan, who always maintains her sense of humor and her faith in me; who is, indeed, my very best friend.

INTRODUCTION

Friday, June 20, 1975, the Congress of the United States: At a hearing in the House of Representatives, Casey Hughes of the National Organization of Women was telling it like it is—40 percent of the labor force is now female; 33 percent of mothers with children under six are working; the number of women with young children who want to work and, in many cases, who need to work if their families are to survive, is increasing every year. In the Senate, at another hearing, the argument was that "the American family is in trouble." To help save it, said some members of Congress and child psychologists, ways should be found to encourage women to stay home and take care of their children.[1]

Meanwhile. . . .

Bob Johnson was in the kitchen of his Chicago home, as he was on most days at about this time, serving a peanut butter and jelly sandwich to his three-year-old son, Ricky, and warming a bottle for ten-month-old Derek. After lunch, he would change Derek's diaper and pack an assortment of child-care necessities—Kimbies, Zwieback, talcum powder, an extra T-shirt—into a canvas bag. He had promised to take Ricky to a local park where, if Derek was kind enough to nap in his carriage, they would be able to go up and down the "big slide" together. And there was marketing to be done if dinner was to be ready by the time Bob's wife, Kathy, was home from her daily rounds as sales representative for a New York publishing house.

In Queens, New York, Roger Gatke was thinking about dinner, too, though not for his wife. He had no wife, had never been married. But he had two adopted sons—nine-year-old Neal and eleven-year-old Tommy—and he was about to adopt his third child, a thirteen-year-old boy whose name was Anthony. Today, after he got off from work, he had to take the boys shopping for sneakers, then get them to the dentist. Both had cavities, so there would be drilling. Their teeth would be sensitive to heat and also to cold. What could he make for dinner?

Steve Hoffman was just getting home from work at 1:00 P.M., having put in four hours at the printing shop he owned in Manhattan. It was time to pick up two-year-old Michael from his morning play group. Steve's wife, Debby, was at the shop, would be for the rest of the afternoon, designing layouts for brochures, jobbing out orders, checking plates. Steve would not return until tomorrow, when it would be Debby's turn to take care of Michael. With the sky overcast, ruling out trips to the zoo or park, the question was what to do for the rest of the afternoon?

Al Dawson, gazing out over a sprawling Los Angeles from the twenty-third floor of an air-conditioned office building, was worried about the backlog of work on his desk. Maybe if he skipped lunch he would be able to finish the budget analysis by 5:00 P.M. He had to leave by then in order to pick up four-year-old Timmy at the day-care center by 6:00 P.M. Al had sought and won custody when he and Sheila divorced. But days like this were hard. There was no one else to pick up

Timmy, and all the boss could think about was the budget. He didn't seem to understand what it was like to raise a child.

Back in Congress that day, there was not one word spoken about the "average" American father, not to mention fathers like Bob, Roger, Steve, or Al. There was no mention of the role of men in child care. It was as if the changing American family consisted only of women and their children.

This is a book about men and child care. Its origins are in a personal experience. In 1968, during my first months of teaching at the Circle Preschool in Oakland, California, I had a recurrently jolting experience. Again and again I found myself being asked the same question: "What do you *really* do?"

It was a question that never would have been asked of a woman. My female colleagues could work with three- and four-year-olds all their lives without anybody expecting that they should—or might—be doing something else. Teaching nursery school was one of the things women often did—when they weren't being homemakers and mothers. But for a man to spend so much time with young children? It was the first time I realized, in any personal sense, just how different the purposes (and personalities) of men and women are expected to be.

Six years later, but largely as an outgrowth of that experience, I began work on this book. The question—"What do you really do?"—had stuck with me, raising my consciousness. I began noticing that other men were, for one reason or another, moving into traditionally female roles, entering into new caring relationships with children at work or at home. Some, like me, who originally selected teaching in preschool or day-care programs as a practical and socially constructive alternative to military service, were staying with it because they enjoyed their work. Others were beginning to renegotiate their family roles; as their wives went out to work, they opted to stay home or to reduce their working time in order to take care of the children. They were not just "helping the wife with the kids," but choosing the personal satisfaction of full-time fatherhood. Single men were adopting children and, in marriages that were breaking up, still others were challenging legal traditions that threatened to deny them, almost automatically, an equal right to child custody.

At a time, then, when many women were struggling for an "equal opportunity" that depended, in part, on freedom from the exclusive constraints of child rearing, some men were seeking "equal opportunity" to take care of children.

Thanks to a grant from the National Affairs Division of the Ford Foundation, I was able to spend a year and a half visiting with a number of these men in various parts of the country. I set out with neither psychological nor sociological theory. I had no questionnaires but, rather, several broad questions to steer my curiosity: Who are these men? Why are they doing what they do? What are the obstacles, if any, that they face—from without and from within? What is life like for them? And how do their lives touch ours?

Initially, I expected to find only a handful of men who met my criteria, much less who would be willing to put up with my observing their lives. I sought them out by contacting friends all over the country who work in some aspect of child care—in day-care centers, nursery schools, social welfare agencies, pediatric clinics. I followed up stories about househusbands and single fathers that appeared, typically, on the "women's pages" of the country's newspapers. And I wrote to the bureau of adoptions in every state. One person led to another. In cities like Boston, Minneapolis, Washington, Portland, Denver, Chicago, Seattle, Los Angeles, Little Rock, and New York, I found myself being referred to "one person you have to interview" who led, naturally, to "another person you must interview," and so on and so on. I began collecting the names of far more people than I could (given the constraints of time and funding) even approach. By the end of eighteen months, I had spoken with more than 120 men, not counting family members, friends, and colleagues. I interviewed some of these people for three or four hours, some for upward of twenty; others, I virtually moved in with—at work or at home—for three or four days at a stretch.

14

During the course of my travels, I spent a good deal of time interviewing and observing men who work as child carers —pediatric nurses, preschool teachers, day-care teachers. I was especially eager to write about this group. Having worked with young children and having encouraged other men to do so, I was aware that "occupational segregation" works two ways in our society, that norms of manliness act as a psychological barrier to keep many men out of traditionally female work. My interest increased when I found that, after explaining to people that I was writing a book about men in primary child-caring roles at work or at home, I kept being introduced as someone who was writing a book about fathers. The teachers and nurses always got left out. It was as if fatherhood were the only frame of reference people had in their heads for thinking about men and children. I was determined to alter that frame of reference.

Eventually, however, I saw I would have to narrow my focus to fatherhood. The subject I had started to investigate was proving to be far greater than I had imagined; concentration on the family would, it seemed, lend my project the necessary coherence. The nuclear family is very much the primary unit in which we raise our children in this society; despite forecasts to the contrary, I do not see it being rejected by large numbers of people. But it is changing. As it changes, as the number of women working outside the home increases, and as the divorce rate soars, the question of *who* will care for the children becomes increasingly important; and child rearing within the nuclear family becomes more obviously a crucial fulcrum for any major change in the roles of men and women.

Our whole society operates, for the most part, on two inter-locking assumptions: that it is the natural role of men to be, first and foremost, breadwinners, and that it is the natural role of women to take care of children. Even as the latter premise is challenged—as more and more women work outside the home—it highlights just how little the former is even questioned. While the United States Department of Labor publishes annual statistics revealing the increase in the number of children with working mothers, government and foundation money spurs research to study the effects on children when their mothers work outside the home. But no national statistics are kept on the number of working fathers, and no research is done into the effects on children when their fathers work, even if these working fathers are so busy that they rarely see their children.

Debate about day care is cast in a language which makes it seem relevant only to the lives of women, even by those of its advocates—like Cornell psychologist Urie Bronfenbrenner—who are most concerned about developing national policies supportive of *family* life: "I think that day care should include a guiding principle, one of allowing the *mother* a freedom of choice so that *she* is not forced either to provide no care for *her* children or, in effect, forced to leave the child in a situation which *she* does not regard as acceptable." [2]

Part-time jobs and flexible scheduling are advocated as a means of enabling women—not men—to combine work outside the home with "family obligations." According to a report from the Organization for Economic Cooperation and Development, part-time work "could give certain women at a certain stage in their existence a feeling of equilibrium." [3] During that certain stage in their existence when men are the parents of young children, there seems to be neither the need for nor the possibility of such a balance.

This neglect of the role—or potential role—of men in child care is not surprising. There is, to be sure, no vocal minority of men clamoring to take on either the responsibilities or the rewards of child rearing. As Marc Feigen Fasteau says in *The Male Machine*, "The rewards of caring for a child are real, but essentially personal, hard to measure or hang on to. This is not the kind of experience men are taught to value. It does not lead to power, wealth, or high status." [4]

To write about men taking care of children is to tap strong and complicated emotions. It is a delicate issue, how we take care of our children. The suggestion that now and in the future more men might choose roles traditionally assigned to women is very threatening to some people. As an editor of a popular women's magazine explained in declining to excerpt any section

16

of this book, "basically the argument that men make as good mothers as women wouldn't make a big hit with our readers."

From women, I have encountered everything from naive surprise at the thought that a man could change diapers to absolute outrage at the fact that men have not been involved more in the daily tasks of caring for children; an outrage expressed in its purist distillation, perhaps, by feminist critic Shulamith Firestone's comment that "the heart of woman's oppression is her childbearing and childrearing roles." [5] From men, too, I have encountered everything from surprise to hostility and defensiveness at any intimation that, for a man, there could be other ways of "taking care" of their families than breadwinning. But I have also encountered from both men and women a readiness to acknowledge that our patterns of child rearing—so deeply ingrained in every aspect of our culture—have limited our notions, and our children's notions, of what it is to be a human being caring for other human beings.

As I know from my travels, and perhaps best of all from my own experience after the birth of my first child, it is not easy to change those patterns. Despite the fact that my wife went back to work part time as a teacher four months after Jessica's birth, despite the fact that she planned to continue an active working life, the assumption was inbred in both of us that she was the primary child rearer, as I was the primary breadwinner. When I took a very demanding job as executive director of a child-care program in a public-housing project, I found myself in the ironic position of spending some twelve hours a day—six or seven days a week—working to ensure that other people's children would have quality child care while I spent very little time at home helping to take care of my daughter, then a very delightful but also demanding toddler. I was depriving myself of an opportunity to know my own child and, in a very real sense, burdening my wife with the double jobs of work and family. It took some slow and difficult reevaluation of the premises that we both brought to our marriage, the expectations we had of each other, to acknowledge how important it is for both of us to work outside the home *and* to be intimately and equally involved in the care of our children.

In this book I have purposely written about men who have *chosen*, within the family context, to take on child-caring roles traditionally thought appropriate for women; about men who sought custody of their children rather than about widowers, even though both may have similar responsibilities as single parents, and about men working part time so as to share child care, even though many men with full-time jobs share equally in bringing up their children. Moreover, I have purposely written about situations that seem to be working: about men, for example, who are satisfied staying home full time rather than about men who have tried staying home and given up in despair, their consciousnesses raised about how awful the homemaker's lot is. This is not to imply that all such situations are workable, but to draw attention to the viability of new options for family life. Nor is this to suggest that men in nontraditional roles are more "caring" in an emotional sense, that they are "better" fathers, or that there is any one "right way" to organize family life or to bring up children. Family dynamics vary widely—as do the needs of individuals and the choices available to them.

For the most part, the choices I am writing about are available to families to be found among the college-educated middle and upper-middle class. A man can afford to reduce his working time only if his wife can earn a complementary income; often he can contest custody only if he is able to afford a substantial legal fee. I do not mean to slight the child caring done by men in the large number of families at lower-income levels where, as I am well aware, economic survival often means a husband's working the night shift and then looking after the children during the day, while his wife is out at work. The small number of families I have written about—in which men have chosen to take on significant caring responsibility for young children—are admittedly a minority phenomenon. But, as such, they highlight more than most the extent to which our society discourages the participation of men in child rearing. At the same time, they will, I hope, point the way to new possibilities—new choices—for men, women, and children.

18

One last point, about the children. Again and again, as people found out about my project, I have been asked, "What effect does it—or will it—have on children to grow up in families with fathers as such significant care givers?"

The question is, of course, a fascinating and important one, but I don't have the answer, at least not in the way most people expect. Mine was not a longitudinal research study, following the growth of children from, say, infancy to adolescence. And I was not interested in "masculinity" or "femininity" or any other arbitrary categories for labeling people, but in the give-and-take of family life, the dailiness of caring for children.

Whenever possible I did try to learn about the child's point of view. While most of the children were too young to talk about their experience, several older ones were well aware that their families were different from the "normal" families they learned about in school or from television, the stereotypic two-parent families in which Father works and Mother stays home full time. It is not easy to grow up in a society that suspects as pathological any variation from this stereotype. Still, even when children knew that their families were different—a result of adoption by a single man or of role reversal—their families were, after all, their families, sources of love and protection, places where people loved one another and had hurt feelings and got angry or laughed, places where people grew.

1

MOTHERS, FATHERS, AND EXPERTS

"Fathers don't make good mothers." So said a New York family court judge in 1975 as he denied a father's petition for custody of his four-year-old son! [1]

It was but one fleeting expression—with consequences more immediately discernible than most—of a belief pervasive in our society: that men and women are biologically destined to play not only different but mutually exclusive roles as parents; that an inherent nurturing ability disposes women to be more interested in and able to care for children than are men; and that for their well-being, children need mothers in a way that they do not need fathers.

"As much as children need a father around when they are growing up," says Dr. Bennett Olshaker, pediatrician and author of the popular child-rearing manual *What Shall We Tell the Kids?* "the need for a mother is of even greater importance, particularly during infancy and preschool years.

21

While mothers may or may not breast feed their babies, the cuddling, closeness, and tactile stimulation that should go with feeding are all very important for the healthy emotional, as well as physical, development of the human being." [2] Presumably, fathers can provide no comparable cuddling or closeness even while they bottle-feed their babies.

Nor should they try, warns Dr. Haim Ginott in his national best-seller *Between Parent and Child:* "In the modern family . . . many men find themselves involved in mothering activities, such as feeding, diapering, and bathing a baby. Though some men welcome these new opportunities for closer contact with their infants, there is the danger that the baby may end up with two mothers, rather than with a mother and a father." [3] Not, significantly, the possibility that the baby might end up with two *parents* who, because they shared such daily tasks, were equally aware of just how difficult, demanding, and gratifying it could be to nurture a young life.

Dr. Bruno Bettelheim urges similar caution:

> Today's father is often advised to participate in infant care as much as the mother does, so that he, too, will be as emotionally enriched as she. Unfortunately, this is somewhat empty advice because the male physiology and that part of his psychology based on it are not geared to infant care. Not that there is anything wrong in a father's giving the baby a bottle. . . . But infant care and child-rearing, unlike choice of work, are not activities in which who should do what can be decided independently of physiology. . . . The relationship between father and child never was and cannot now be built principally around child-caring experiences. It is built around a man's function in society: moral, economic, political. [4]

It is hardly possible to measure the impact of such statements, for—along with countless others—they permeate our lives no less than the air we breathe. On the one hand, it seems, they simply describe the differing roles taken by most men and women in bringing up their young children. On the other hand, however, they help sustain those roles, providing a "scientific" rationale to buttress the popular belief that our dominant child-rearing patterns reflect some natural order.

But is there such a natural order? Are there innate biological differences in the ability of men and women to nurture their young?

According to Harvard anthropologist Beatrice Whiting, who has spent a lifetime studying child-rearing practices in cultures around the world, "Attempting to distinguish the relative importance of biology and culture in determining the nurturing behavior of men and women is not worth your while. You will find that research in this area is like a can of worms." We were sitting in Dr. Whiting's Cambridge home as she issued this warning, "Don't even bother with social science in your book. Stick to the lives of real people. You don't need scientific studies to show how various human lives can be, to show that men can take care of children."

Dr. Whiting was correct, I think, on both counts. The bulk of this book is about real lives, about some of the ways in which our social norms restrict human variety, and about ways in which these norms are loosening—and might be loosened further—to allow men and women more room to express their personal selves. Still, social science cannot be neglected. In a society that relies so heavily on "experts," it is important to realize that what the experts tell us depends largely on the questions they ask—on the questions they consider important (or possible) to ask. And what the record shows is that the experts have asked very few questions about men and children, that their research has proceeded for the most part to confirm popular assumptions without even questioning them. Taking as a premise that woman means "nurturer" and man means "breadwinner," social scientists have hardly been able to entertain the idea—until recently—that both mother and father mean "parent."

The bias is long-standing, of course. Whether or not they derived their orientation from Freud—who described the mother-infant relationship as "the root of the mother's importance, unique, without parallel, established unalterably for the whole lifetime as the first and strongest love-object, and as the prototype of all later love relations—for both sexes"—researchers and theorizers about child development have, almost without exception, emphasized the uniqueness of the infant's relationship with its mother.[5]

Perhaps the most influential modern claim for innate differences in the abilities of mothers and fathers to meet the needs of their young children comes from the work of British psychoanalyst and ethologist John Bowlby, who, starting in the late 1940's, did pioneering studies of infant-mother interaction. Bowlby was concerned, in particular, with the mental health of children who were deprived of such interaction, children being raised in orphanages, hospitals, or other institutions. His 1951 report to the World Health Organization, *Maternal Care and Mental Health,* did much to improve the care of such children. However, even though institutionalized children were deprived of both mothers and fathers (or simply of constant care givers), Bowlby focused exclusively on the mother. In a now classic paper of 1959, "The Nature of the Child's Tie to His Mother," and in his subsequent work, Bowlby postulated that there were deep psychological roots to motherliness and that the newborn child had an innate or instinctual disposition to relate to its mother, and *only* to its mother. The helpless child needed protection from an adult, and that adult, reasoned Bowlby, was the mother; the child had to stay in close proximity to the mother lest it die.

But the relationship was symbiotic. In effect, the very presence of the child activated in the mother a potential for nurturant response that ensured the formation of a mother-child bond, the basis for healthy emotional development. To upset the mother-child bond was to intervene with a fundamental dynamic in species survival; to prevent the child's natural tendency to "attach" to the mother was to run the risk of abnormal development. As Bowlby said, "When deprived of maternal care, the child's development is almost always retarded—physically, intellectually, and socially. . . ." [6]

The implication of Bowlby's position was that men had no innate "fatherliness," and newborns no propensity to "attach" to their fathers; if they did, men would be at home, impelled by the laws of nature to ensure species survival. The role of the male in the child-rearing process was, according to Bowlby, to support the bond between mother and child. "Fathers have their uses even in infancy. Not only do they provide for their wives to enable them to devote themselves unrestrictedly to the care of the infant and toddler, but, by providing love and companionship, they support her emotionally and help her maintain that harmonious contented mood in the aura of which the infant thrives." [7]

As long ago as 1953, Dr. Margaret Mead suggested that any claim for an innate nurturing potential in women, or for a biologically rooted dependence of children on their mothers alone, was suspect of being "a new and subtle form of anti-feminism in which men—under the guise of exalting the importance of maternity—are tying women more tightly to their children." [8] Dr. Mead had reason to believe, from her own studies of primitive societies, like the Arapesh of New Guinea —where it was quite normal for men to share fully in the care of infants—that culture, not biology, dictated child-rearing practices. Nevertheless, research into child development proceeded in the 1950's and 1960's with an almost singular fixation on the relationships between children and their mothers, with Bowlby's hypothesis providing a guiding framework. Indeed, as the number of working mothers with young children began to increase, so did the amount of investigation into the possible effects of maternal deprivation. As sociologist Leonard Benson says, "When women work, most students are alerted at once to the unavoidable family implications. Only the work of men is isolable from domestic matters. . . ." [9]

It was not until the rebirth of feminism in the late 1960's that both the popular version of the motherhood mystique and the scientific concentration on "maternal deprivation" came under a sustained attack. What Dr. Mead had called the exalted importance of maternity was not only tying women to their children but strangling *both* in the process. For women to be free as individuals, to have balanced lives and equal opportunity with men, freedom from exclusive child-rearing responsibilities (and from the household work that went with it) was necessary; and that meant, in some way, freedom from the guilt-inducing myth that they were inherently and solely capable—as men were not—of caring for the young child. As Angela Barron McBride, a psychiatric nurse and mother of two, argued in *The Growth and Development of Mothers*, "Because a women has functioning mammary glands, it does not logically follow that she should forever be responsible for the nurturing needs (or the cooking, for that matter) of the entire family. . . . There is something both dangerous and ridiculous about inferring social norms from physiological functioning." [10]

What evidence is there that the ability to carry a child in the womb or any other aspect of female physiology predisposes women to care for children? Are there hormones, for example, that "prime" women to respond to their newborns?

According to Stanford psychologists Eleanor Emmons Maccoby and Carol Nagy Jacklin, coauthors of *The Psychology of Sex Differences,* as of 1975 the most comprehensive and authoritative review of research on sex differences, such hormones are found among rats, but "Little is known concerning the possible basis of maternal behavior in species higher than rodents." [11] And, as Yale psychologist Michael Lamb reminds us, the role of hormones seems to decrease as one ascends the phylogenetic scale: "There is every reason to believe that among humans societal prescriptions are *at least* as important in the regulation of parental behavior, and are probably far more important. There is no reason to believe that hormones are either necessary or sufficient conditions for the display of human parental behavior." [12]

Indeed, videotapes of mothers interacting with newborns at the National Center for Child Abuse Prevention in Denver indicate that the responsiveness of mothers to infants varies dramatically, and depends very much on the mother's feelings about herself. Some mothers seem, almost "instinctively," to fondle their offspring, to coo at them, and to make frequent eye-to-eye contact; but others—often with unwanted pregnancies, bad marriages, or dire poverty to return to—seem, also "instinctively," to reject their babies, refusing to look at or touch them and, in some cases, threatening murder.

What about the female ability to lactate? Isn't that evidence that, no matter what their feelings or initial responses, women are uniquely qualified to meet the needs of young children?

"Mothers may be particularly sensitive to the needs of

their babies," writes Dr. Rochelle Wortis in the *American Journal of Orthopsychiatry*.

> However, it is also true that a woman who has just had her first child, and who has not previously handled, fed, or cared for an infant, has great difficulty in the first days of the baby's life in establishing feeding, whether it be by breast or bottle. New mothers often have to be told how to hold the baby, burp it, bathe it, and dress it. Of course, most women learn how to care for their infants quite efficiently within a short period of time, through practice and determination.[13]

And in a modern industrial society, it is hard to argue that the uniquely female ability to breast-feed is essential for survival of the species: twenty years ago, a generation of American infants was raised on bottles because the medical profession thought cow's milk or prepared formula healthier than mother's milk.

None of this is to deny the uniqueness of the relationship between mother and child. "Mothering a newborn infant is a singular activity, like no other in human experience," says Mary C. Howell, M.D., Ph.D., assistant professor of pediatrics at Harvard Medical School.[14] But, argues Dr. Howell, herself the mother of six,

> it should be noted immediately that many or most of the essential aspects of "mothering" might better be considered as aspects of "parenting." . . . Nurturing of the human young rests, in large part, in adapting to the changing educability of the immature creature cared for. This responsiveness to the child requires a flexibility characteristic of learned, rather than instinctive, behavior. The near-exclusive assignment of functional parenting to women is a condition of our society that is not universally shared by all human societies, nor even by all primate groups. We should, therefore, remember that the child care usually performed by mothers might be just as well carried out by fathers.[15]

What about fathers? To behavioral scientists, they have been, until recently, almost a nonexistent species. In 1958 a major sociological study of the American family entitled *The*

Changing American Parent appeared, based on interviews with 582 *mothers.* It was not unique. Major studies of American parents by well-respected psychologists and sociologists reveal the same phenomenon again and again: to write *Patterns of Child Rearing,* psychologist Robert Sears and his colleagues at Stanford University interviewed 379 "parents"—all of them mothers; Robert Blood and Donald Wolfe based their classic study, *Husbands and Wives: The Dynamics of Married Living,* on interviews with 909 mothers and no fathers; and in a major study of divorced parents, sociologist William Goode talked with 425 mothers and not one father.[16]

Even when a study entitled "Father Participation in Infancy" appeared in 1969—one of the very first to acknowledge the possibility of interactions between men and their very young children—the authors admitted, with commendable honesty and obvious embarrassment, that the study might have been better if they had actually observed the fathers, or even talked to them. "It causes [us] great embarrassment," said Frank A. Pedersen, Ph.D., and Kenneth S. Robson, M.D., "to report that the actual data on father participation were secured by interviewing the mothers. Perhaps we did not have the courage of our own convictions to do a proper observational study or reorient our work schedules to coincide with the availability of fathers." [17]

Indeed, the first study to rely on direct laboratory observations of interactions between fathers and their young children was not done until 1970, when Harvard Ph.D. student Milton Kotelchuck set out to do a thesis with a title—"The Nature of the Child's Tie to His Father"—that ironically mimicked Bowlby. So few studies of fathers and infants interacting had been done by then that Kotelchuck claims, "It took me a half hour to review all the literature. And I read the full articles, not the abstracts!" He was not exaggerating. A survey of family research found that, in 444 papers published between 1963 and 1968, only eleven relied on data from husbands or fathers; in 1,141 pages of text, the *Handbook of Socialization Theory and Research* makes only five specific references to fathers; and Leonard Carmichael's *Manual of Child Psychology,* the standard reference work in the field, does not even list fathers in the index.[18]

Even when they have tried to assess the effect of fathers on child development, researchers have, by and large, adopted an approach that assumes it normal for men *not* to interact with their children. Ignoring any routine, if minimal, child care done by men, they focus instead on "father absence." And they define "father absence" as occurring, not in families where fathers are constantly working overtime or away on business trips, but only when men are separated from their children by divorce, death, or wartime service. Unlike the research on maternal deprivation—which often includes children of women who are working, sometimes part time—research on father absence displays an almost singular interest in the development of male sex-role identity in the son of an "absent" father.

For example, after reviewing the literature on father absence, Dr. Henry Biller concludes, "There is evidence that the young father-absent boy is more dependent, less aggressive, and less competent in peer relations than his father-present counterpart. He seems likely to have an unmasculine self-concept." [19] Biller's statement is typical in its implication that there is some objective and normative state of masculinity that fathers transmit to their sons. But just what masculinity is— and whether it is a good thing to have, whether it enhances the ability of a male to function healthily in our society—is rarely examined. If, for example, an "unmasculine self-concept" means warmth, kindness, and sensitivity to others rather than machismo, is this a sign of deviance? [20] By narrowing their concern to the father's effect on stereotypical sex-role identity—and the "absent" father at that—researchers have implicitly emphasized attention to differences between the roles of men and women in child rearing, without making any room for attention to similarities; they have promoted the notion that women—and women only—could be nurturant care givers.

Now a convergence of forces is prompting behavioral scientists to begin taking a fresh look at the male parent. The women's movement is unquestionably the most powerful; as it has raised questions about the way culture shapes female behavior—and about the way scientists have concentrated on the mother-child relationship—so it has inevitably begun to raise questions about the way culture shapes male behavior, and about the way scientists have neglected father-child relationships. Moreover, the women's movement has begun to make a once far-fetched question more plausible: If both men and women prepare for full-time employment, who *will* raise the children? From a practical point of view, the increasing number of men who are "coaching" the labor and delivery of their children is giving researchers a new pool of subjects and has made father-newborn interaction a "researchable" topic.

While there is hardly a coherent body of research about men and children, studies done so far are highly provocative. In a Cincinnati hospital, for example, when fathers and mothers were given an equal chance to hold their babies in the first few days after birth, fathers were more likely than mothers to hold and visually attend to their infants.[21] At a time when such studies are rare, some researchers make it sound as if they have discovered a new creature—it doesn't lactate and it doesn't have a uterus, but it shows a surprisingly warm response to its offspring!

For example, Drs. Martin Greenberg and Norman Morris, observing father reactions to their two- and three-day-old infants, report that

> The fathers enjoy looking at their own baby as opposed to other babies and perceive the newborn to be attractive, pretty, or beautiful. . . . There is a desire for and pleasure of tactile contact with the newborn. . . . In spite of some of the so-called unsightly aspects and awkwardness of the baby, the infant is seen by many as the epitome of perfection. . . . Many of the fathers have reported themselves to be so moved by the impact of the newborn that they feel drawn in toward the baby as if it were a magnet. Their attraction to the newborn is very powerful, and it appears to be something over which they have no control. They do not will it to happen; it just does.[22]

30

Drs. Greenberg and Morris hypothesize that there is a "basic, innate potential among all fathers" to be "engrossed" by their newborns, that this potential is elicited by the presence of the newborn, and that "the greater the early physical contact with the infant, the more likely it is that engrossment will occur.[23] In effect, the conjectures of Greenberg and Morris give an ironic twist to the biological determinist position of John Bowlby; Greenberg and Morris are warning of the dangers, not of a maternal deprivation whereby the infant is denied contact with its mother, but of a paternal deprivation where the father is denied contact with the infant. They are saying that our child-rearing practices—hospital procedures that don't allow men to be with their newborn and a culture which, in general, deems it unmanly for a father to reveal a "motherly" interest in his babies—are likely to prevent the engrossment phenomenon from occurring, perhaps impairing the biologically based responsiveness that men have to their children.

Research into the experiences of men before the birth of their children—during the pregnancy period—is also calling for a reexamination of old assumptions. In general, writings about pregnancy, birth, and postpartum infant care have either ignored men or emphasized the emotional crises that some men have as they become fathers; the literature discloses titles like "Pregnancy as a Precipitant of Mental Illness in Men," "Fatherhood as a Precipitant of Mental Illness," "Paranoid Psychoses Associated with Impending or Newly Established Fatherhood." [24] Male symptoms associated with pregnancy—like nausea, weight gain, toothache, and so forth—have often been considered among signs of pathology.

Now, however, some researchers are hypothesizing that emphasis on pathology has led to a misinterpretation of male symptoms during pregnancy and has obscured exploration of the ways in which the birth of a child can be, for a man as well as for a woman, a time of deep personal enrichment, a time that activates healthy desires to share in the nurturing of life. Indeed, when a research team in Boston compared two groups of expectant fathers—one with and one without pregnancy "symptoms"—it found that "the symptom group was

31

rated as more positive about their wives' pregnancies, [and] participated much more in child care. . . ." [25] According to psychologist Robert Fein, it may be that the suppression of healthy desires to share, by a culture which teaches men not to express their emotions during pregnancy (or any other time) and which excludes men from labor and delivery, results in symptom formation.[26]

At the same time that the reactions of fathers to their infants are being reexamined, so are the reactions of infants to their fathers. According to Dr. Milton Kotelchuck, who did the pioneering study "The Nature of the Child's Tie to His Father" as his Ph.D. dissertation, "I think of my work as pointing out the obvious, that the infant's ties to its parents are not based on the sex of the parent." Kotelchuck compared the reactions of 144 children ranging in age from six to twenty-one months when either their mother or their father, or both, walked out of his laboratory playroom, leaving them with a stranger. "Most previous experiments of this type," says Kotelchuck, "by comparing only [the infant's reaction to] the mother and a stranger, came to the misleading conclusion that the mother's relationship seems somehow special or unique." [27] In his experiment, however, most infants protested equally the departure of father or mother. "When another familiar person is introduced, such as the father, the presumed uniqueness of the mother-child relationship seems to disappear . . . it became obvious that fathers are indeed important to their infants." [28]

While there have been no studies done of men actually taking care of children for sustained periods, a provocative study that is worth looking at was done with rhesus monkeys —a species in which mothers are extremely protective of their young and in which adult males have usually been observed in the wild as detached, indifferent, and sometimes hostile to infants. Psychologists William Redican, Gary Mitchell, and Jody Gomber of the University of California at Davis took month-old infant monkeys away from their mothers and placed them in cages with adult males. They hypothesized that free-ranging males do not show "paternalness" because they rarely have a "reasonable opportunity to display and develop a set of parental-care behaviors.[29] Because of past reports of infanticide by adult males, they carefully familiarized the animals with each other before bringing them together, and protected the infants from unexpected and possibly fatal aggression. The researchers' findings confirmed their original premise: the adult males, once accustomed to the playful poking and biting of their infant cage mates, displayed a far greater range of caregiving behavior than had ever been observed. They not only groomed the infants, but played with them more frequently—and in a more sustained way—than did female monkeys raising their infants alone. At the end of seven months, when his "baby" was removed from the cage for two days, an adult male named Mellon "raged and bit himself so severely that he cut several major blood vessels in his leg. He would have died if he had not received veterinary treatment." [30]

Redican, Mitchell, and Gomber are quick to point out that monkeys are not human beings in fur suits; to extrapolate directly from one species to another can be dangerous; but it is equally dangerous, they argue, not to recognize the questions that their research poses for human beings: "If adult male rhesus monkeys, characterized as indifferent or even hostile to infants in the wild, can become intimately attached to them in the laboratory, what might this augur for man?" They continue,

> The biological basis for assigning social roles comes into serious question. . . . On the basis of some form of biological imperative, mothers have often been assigned not only a sufficient but a necessary role in rearing offspring. Our research has uncovered a substantial potential for nurturant parental care in as relatively inflexible a creature as the male rhesus monkey. This seems to offer some promise for the human male, the hallmark of whose species is behavioral plasticity. In a sense, we have tried to rebut a *negative* argument that, because of innate factors, males cannot form close attachments with infants. Human males are a rich resource which can be tapped during this period of changing social and sex roles.
>
> While men and women generally behave differently, the important fact is that a particular man and a woman may not. While men and women are becoming less different or per-

haps different in a new way, we should try to discover the biocultural potential for both sexes. But more importantly, we should allow individuals to discover their own biocultural potential, regardless of their assigned sex.[31]

As scientists like Redican, Mitchell, and Gomber begin to speculate, there is a quiet and steady increase in the number of men who are indeed challenging our socially assigned roles for child rearing. Perhaps they are discovering their "biocultural potential." If so, they are also finding out how hard our society works to discourage its expression. And they are showing all of us that, whatever the nurturing potential of any person, actually taking responsibility for the dailiness of a child's life can be fascinating, frustrating, enervating, and exhilarating—that it is fraught with all the contradictions of human caring.

2

CONFRONTING FATHERHOOD: MEN AND CUSTODY

THE MATERNAL PRESUMPTION

Pretend that it is 1971 and you are a young attorney, just graduated from Harvard Law School and returned home to Minneapolis to establish your practice. An old high-school classmate calls (he's heard you're back in town) to ask if you will represent him in a divorce. The important thing, he says, is that he wants custody of his two young children. You are sorry to hear that his marriage has not worked out well, you say, and set up an appointment to see him. You have never handled a divorce case before, so, before he arrives, you consult a guidebook on family law published by the Family Law Committee of the Minnesota State Bar Association, where you receive the following advice about your potential client:

> Except in very rare cases, the father should not have the custody of the minor children of the parties. He is usually un-

qualified psychologically and emotionally; nor does he have the time and care to supervise the children. A lawyer not only does an injustice to himself, but he is unfair to his client, to the state, and to society if he gives any encouragement to the father that he should have custody of his children. A lawyer who encourages his client to file for custody, unless it is one of the classic exceptions, has difficulty collecting his fees, has a most unreasonable client, has taken the time of the court and the welfare agencies involved, and has put a burden on his legal brethren.[1]

As prejudicial as it sounds, this counsel to the young lawyer is but an extremist's distillation from a legal system in which, for the most part, a father has nothing close to equal rights when it comes to custody of his children. "You go to one lawyer and he tells you that you probably don't stand a chance," says a divorced man from New York, "so you go to another one. He tells you the same thing. And then a third confirms it. Just think of it like going to the doctor for a diagnosis. Three doctors, three experts, all tell you the same thing. What do you do?"

With every instance of divorce in which the custody of children is an issue, a man realizes—perhaps for the first time in his life—that he can be denied something other than the ladies' room because of his sex. Whatever ties he has with his children may well be broken, or affected substantially, because he is a male. Divorce is an experience that pulls a man up short, forcing him to examine just what he has been like as a father, just what connections, if any, he has with his children's lives, what sort of a loss it will be to them if, in fact, he becomes one of the breed he's encountered so often—the weekend father. It is an experience that makes a man realize with shocking suddenness what the personal costs are of living in a society that considers child rearing to be the function of women.

Here, for example, is Alan Geller, who, along with his wife, Anne, made the same decision in 1973 as one out of every three couples: "The marriage is over."

I was supposed to do the manly, gentlemanly thing—to move out. I didn't really want to, but her rationalization was that the kids didn't have any examples of mothers moving out. Fifty percent of their friends are from families with a separation or divorce; but in all those cases, the man moves out. So I agreed initially, and the children were told I was moving out. They even went with me to look for a new apartment. But sometimes in the middle of the night, I'd wake with a terrible feeling in my guts: What was I doing? It was all a contrivance! I was as central in my children's lives as she was. I knew it, she knew it, and they knew it. I was falling into that old trap. I was consecrating the relationship between woman and child. Is there anything inalienable in that 'bond' between woman and child? A father invests or can invest as much life in a child; there's nothing in principle, in psychology or biology, that excludes that from happening. It's not preordained that a father invests less life in a child.

Not preordained but so thoroughly ingrained in our system of jurisprudence that, according to legal scholars Henry Foster and Doris Jonas Freed, regardless of state laws stipulating that the "best interests of the child"—not parental sex—shall be the determining factor in custody disputes, "due to the mystique of motherhood, the mother has the advantage and, except in the most unusual cases, will be awarded custody when she seeks it, unless there is a strong showing of unfitness or abandonment . . . in effect many of the decisions tacitly imply that the father's claim to custody as against the mother's is slightly, if any, better than that of an utter stranger." [2]

Witness this 1974 case from Massachusetts, where the law states, "The rights of the parents shall, in the absence of misconduct, be held to be equal, and the happiness and the welfare of the children shall determine their custody or possession." [3] A probate court awarded custody of a three-year-old (whom I shall call Jane Rice) to her mother over her father's objections—among them that the child was frequently chain-locked in the bedroom by her mother. Within the following year and a half, Jane was admitted once to the hospital for severe food poisoning and once with a broken leg and an injured heel after being struck by an automobile while crossing the street unattended on an errand for her mother. When Jane was released from the hospital, doctors instructed her mother about bandaging and caring for her. Ten days later, Jane was returned to the hospital on her father's insistence. Her condition was bad—a urine-soaked cast, lice in her hair, and the injured heel badly enough deteriorated to require subsequent skin grafting—so bad that hospital personnel filed a child-abuse complaint against Mrs. Rice and obtained a court order holding Jane in the hospital until an investigation could be completed.

The hospital social worker and an independent psychiatrist found the mother's home unsanitary and unhealthy. A district court reviewed the facts and ordered that Jane be taken from her mother and given to Family and Children's Services, as required by law, pending a determination of proper placement. A team of investigators from Family and Children's Services found that the father's home provided a fit and healthy environment; Jane's father and grandmother could—and wanted to—take care of her. Regardless of these findings, and regardless of subsequent recommendations by the hospital social worker, the independent psychiatrist, and other witnesses that Jane be placed in custody with her father, she was placed by the court, at age four, not with the father, who wanted her all along, but in a foster home with "utter strangers."

Consider another case, from Utah, which in 1975 was the only state to maintain by *statute* that in a custody determination "the court shall consider the best interest of the child . . . and the natural presumption that the mother is best suited to care for young children." [4] The circumstances are taken as *alleged* by attorneys from the American Civil Liberties Union in their presentation to the United States Supreme Court. [5] When David and Edwina Arends separated, they agreed that he would take custody of their seventeen-month-old daughter, Kimberly; Mrs. Arends was, according to her own testimony, depressed and mentally ill. Even before the separation, though, David had assumed primary responsibility for Kimberly, taking exclusive care of her during the daytime, when he returned from his nighttime shift and his wife went to work at her daytime job. Following the separation, David changed jobs, working a shift from 7:00 A.M. to 3:30 P.M., and retaining a middle-aged woman —a professional nurse—to care for Kimberly during the day.

Two years later, when Kimberly was three and a half years old, a trial court ordered her custody transferred to the mother. There was no indication that the father was doing an inadequate job; in fact, the court order modifying custody noted that the father "is still competent to care for said child and has adequate living facilities, etc., for the care of said child." There was no indication that Kimberly was unhappy, or wanted to leave her father's care. However, Mrs. Arends' psychotherapist, who said that she had been "nearly psychotic" a year before and was "still under stress . . . compulsive and somewhat suspicious," recommended that custody be transferred, as did a vocational counselor who, after seeing Mrs. Arends for six sessions, said she had "improved considerably." Neither the therapist nor the counselor ever had any contact with Kimberly or her father.

Whether or not Edwina Arends was less qualified to care for Kimberly than her husband did not matter; nor did it matter that Kimberly had spent almost all of her three and a half years with her father as the primary care giver. According to the law, unless a mother was shown to be totally unfit, she was entitled to custody, no matter what the circumstances. David Arends appealed to the Utah Supreme Court, arguing that the maternal presumption violated his constitutional rights to equal protection and due process, and that a sex-based custody award flouted his daughter's best interest and denied her due process. In a decision that was denied an appellate hearing by the United States Supreme Court, the Utah Supreme Court not only stuck to the letter of the law but embellished it, commenting that the father's constitutional "contention might have some merit to it in a proper case if the father was equally gifted in lactation as is the mother." [6]

It has not always been legal practice to award child custody almost automatically to the mother. Under the English common law, which regarded both women and children as men's "chattels," fathers had what amounted to absolute right to the custody of their children; in 1804, for example, an

39

English court vindicated a father who literally snatched his eight-month-old son from the breast of his estranged wife, carrying him away naked in the middle of the night.[7] It is difficult to define with precision the point in case law when all vestiges of common-law paternalism had disappeared. (As recently as 1926, for example, a review of custody procedures in the *Indiana Law Journal* noted that "the father has a slight advantage over the mother . . . to make use of the ordinary legal phraseology, the father will be preferred over the mother if all things are equal." However, five years earlier a family court in Wisconsin awarded custody to a mother reasoning that "nothing can be an adequate substitute for mother love—for that special ministration required during the period of nurture she can give. . . . The difference between fatherhood and motherhood in this respect is fundamental.") [8]

According to most legal scholars, an opinion written by Chief Justice Brewer of the Supreme Court of Kansas in 1889 set the precedent for making the rights of fathers and mothers equal, and subordinate to the rights of the child. "Above all things," said Justice Brewer in words that underlie all subsequent custody decisions, "the paramount consideration is, what will promote the welfare of the child?" [9] In reality, however, the best interests of the child—especially the child of so-called "tender years," had already become synonymous with mother. By the latter part of the nineteenth century, court decisions were well on their way to promulgating the notion that women had a unique right—and obligation—to take custody. As the United States Supreme Court put it in an 1872 ruling: "The constitution of the family organization, which is founded in the divine ordinance, as well as the nature of things, indicates the domestic sphere as that which properly belongs to the domain of womanhood. . . . The paramount destiny and mission of women are to fulfill the noble and benign offices of wife and mother. This is the law of the Creator." [10]

Since that opinion was written, over a hundred years ago, judges have become far less likely to invoke the law of the Creator than they are to call upon the testimony of professionals—psychiatrists, psychologists, and social workers—who have been trained to understand the dynamics of child development. Psychological training, however, no more occurs in a cultural vacuum than does legal training. Scientific bias has often educated professionals to the belief that women are inherently suited for child rearing, that children need mothers in order to develop optimally, and that women need children in order to be secure in their personal identities. A recent "impartial" investigation by a psychiatric social worker from a Massachusetts court, for example, *began* with the social worker saying to the father (who happened to be chief of psychiatry at a local hospital), "I have to tell you before I begin asking questions that I just don't have the heart to take a child away from its mother."

Less sentimental but with the same effect is the opinion of Dr. Andrew Watson, a psychiatrist and legal scholar who has urged the adoption of a "psychological best interests of the child test," further described as "an organizing concept which can relate and integrate all relevant data in relation to custodial disposition." [11] The test must, of course, be applied on a case-by-case basis, but as a general rule, Dr. Watson does not for one minute question the maternal presumption: "Which parent they need most will vary according to age and, of course, according to the sex of the child. It has become traditional for mothers to be the parent of first choice for children below the age of adolescence. This is psychologically sound provided that the mother is emotionally capable." [12]

Psychologically sound according to what criteria? Aside from tradition, what scientific basis is there for any guidelines which discriminate—even implicitly—against the custody rights of fathers? An attempt to answer the question was made in 1969 when the National Conference of Commissioners on Uniform State Laws was drafting the Uniform Marriage and Divorce Act, the most far-reaching effort in the nation's history to arrive at a national standard regarding divorce and custody. The Conference charged Professor Robert J. Levy, a legal scholar from the University of Minnesota, and Phoebe C. Ellsworth, a social psychologist from Stanford University, with the task of assessing what social scientists have discovered about custodial arrangements and their consequences; we must explore what is empirically known about the differential effects on the child's development of awarding custody, let us say, to the mother rather than to the father, or to some third party rather than to either of the parents. With that information as essential background, we can turn to the task of formulating sound custody adjudication doctrines.[13]

After an exhaustive review of all the research done on divorce, broken homes, father separation and father absence, remarriage and stepparenthood, and maternal deprivation, Levy and Ellsworth concluded:

> As must be painfully clear, the psychological research that can be considered both relevant and useful to the problems of custody adjudication is minimal. Direct studies of the effects of different types of custody arrangement are non-existent. Indirect studies may alert the judge to the hazards in the path of the child of divorce, but cannot indicate whether or in what circumstances a father or a mother is a "better" custodian—at least in part because of the paucity of data on mother-absent families.[14]

Nevertheless, as these scholars noted, if a national policy on custody adjudication was to be adopted, "Choices will have to be made whether or not social science has provided sufficient relevant data to inform them." [15] Their review of the research would seem to call for a recommendation that judges make such choices on a case-by-case basis, with preference given to neither parent because of sex.

But Levy and Ellsworth did not make such a recommendation. The tenacity of tradition is perhaps nowhere more apparent than in the guidelines they offered for the Uniform Marriage and Divorce Act:

> The trial judge's most common task is deciding whether to prefer the father or the mother as custodian of the children. A uniform divorce act should contain a presumption that the mother is the appropriate custodian—at least for young children, and probably for children of any age. We know that custody is usually awarded to the mother—with *ample justification* and very frequently with the husband's acquiescence: . . .

Since wives will, under most circumstances, be awarded custody regardless of the statutory standard, and since it seems wise to discourage traumatic custody contests whenever it is possible to do so, the act should discourage those few husbands who might wish to contest by establishing a presumption that the wife is entitled to custody. The presumption resolves several value conflicts: it may well be true that because of the presumption some fathers who would be better custodians than their wives will either fail to seek custody or will be denied custody following a contest, but that disadvantage has a lower "social cost" than the disadvantages of any alternative statutory formulation—more contested cases (with the trauma that contests seem to produce), more risk of a custody award to a father who will be only marginally better than the mother or even much worse.[16]

These are chilling words, for they perpetuate the belief that it is the role of women—and women alone—to bear the responsibility for child rearing, at the same time that they categorically deny the rights of fathers. And they do so under the guise of protecting children—children like Kimberly Arends and Jane Rice—from trauma.

Had the recommendations of Levy and Ellsworth been adopted by the Conference and proposed (much less implemented) as law, the country might have seen its first class action suit brought by fathers. For, despite the bias of tradition—and despite the advice from their lawyers that they don't stand a chance—more and more men are seeking custody of their children. There are no reliable statistics available to document the phenomenon. (According to sociologist Kelin Gersick, "While there are few jurisdictions that keep adequate statistics, those that do usually report about 5 percent of divorce cases involve a dispute between the husband and wife for custody of the children. This amounts to over 30,000 cases a year in the United States, a conservative estimate, and it seems to be going up."[17]) However, many attorneys practicing family law unhesitatingly recognize the trend in their own practice; according to ACLU attorney Rena K. Uviller, "We get an increasing number of calls from men who want to know if it's legally possible for them to get custody. Many of them have the impression that they have no rights under the law; that's just not true, whatever the bias in practice."

It is not just in isolated instances that men are seeking custody of their children. "Fathers' rights" groups are springing up all over the country. What started in Boston as a group of six divorced men meeting to share their problems grew, from 1973 to 1975, into a 600-member organization called Fathers United for Equal Justice which provides men legal and emotional support and watchdogs judges of particular prejudice (in one case helping to bring about the transfer of four-year-old Jane Rice from a foster home to her father's home). Offshoots of Fathers United have been established in New Hampshire, Rhode Island, and southern California. Chicago has Divorced Men. Northern California has Equal Rights for Fathers. Maryland has Fathers United for Equal Rights and more recently, Equal Rights in Divorce for Children, Men, and Women Through Education and Assistance, which grew, like most, out of one man's personal experience. (Tony Minner, an airline pilot, founded the group in 1973 after a Maryland court concluded, in his divorce case, that "both parents are fit persons to have custody" and then ordered him to transfer custody of his three children to his wife.[18]

But it is not just as advocates for men that these groups profess to be forming. According to Bob LeClaire, vice-president of Fathers United for Equal Justice, "As an organization, we are not against women; we are against a dehumanizing system. And we are trying to reform that system."

The legal system is starting to respond, albeit unevenly, to the rights of children and fathers. Between 1969 and 1975, nine states passed legislation explicitly stipulating that sex of the parent shall not be a factor in determining custody. Florida's new statute, for example, says "the father of the child shall be given the same consideration as the mother." [19]

Changes in statute may do little to affect the practice of judges who say, as reported in one case, "I was raised by my mother and I don't see why other people shouldn't be raised by their mothers." However, there are a growing number of cases in which judges are issuing thoughtful opinions about the maternal presumption. In 1973, Judge George W. Draper II of the Superior Court of the District of Columbia awarded custody to a father, reasoning that custody should go to "the individual (or parent) who fulfills most adequately, the *mothering function*, i.e., the nurturing (physical, emotional, and psychological) which a child needs to become a well-adjusted individual in our society." [20]

Reasoning along similar lines, though in an opinion which goes farther than any earlier opinions in broaching the relevant constitutional issues, Judge Sybil Hart Kooper, of the Family Court of New York, wrote:

> The simple fact of being a mother does not, by itself, indicate a capacity or willingness to render a quality of care different from that which the father can provide. The traditional and romantic view, at least since the turn of the century, has been that nothing can be an adequate substitute for mother love. . . . Later decisions have recognized that this view is inconsistent with informed application of the best interests of the child doctrine and out of touch with contemporary thought about child development and male and female stereotypes. [21]

Even as such enlightened opinions emerge, however, the route to establishing custody remains an ugly one, necessitating in most cases that a man prove his wife unfit as a mother. The adversary system is unsparing. When a prominent attorney from Phoenix was asked to represent a lifetime friend in a custody battle, he declined with the following comment: "We've known each other for a long time, George, but you've never seen me in a courtroom. You don't want to start by seeing me in there with you and Alice. Once I go in there, I'm a different person. I go for blood." Regardless of the outcome, both parents can be destroyed.

"Emotionally, no matter how long this lasts," says a man who won custody, "you're constantly reminded, you're constantly looking for things to enhance your case. You have to keep all these sordid pieces of information in your mind or jot them down so you don't forget them. It's like preparing yourself a hundred times before the trial to make sure you're ready." Whatever dirt exists is dredged up. "I feel rotten about it," says a man still involved in a custody battle. "But that's what you have to do."

Why do it? Why pursue custody? It is a question that comes up, again and again—a question rarely put to women. For it is commonly assumed that, as a matter of nature, all women want custody, that no "good mother" would consider giving up her children (such assumptions force some women into fighting for custody even if they really don't want it). Conversely, it is readily assumed that men seek custody only to antagonize their wives; for example, on their way to recommending that a uniform divorce act should contain a presumption in favor of the mother, Levy and Ellsworth noted, "It is well known that many husbands who seek custody of their young children do so as part of a general vendetta against their wives." [22]

But there is no simple answer to the question of why some men seek custody. In the case of divorce, where animosities run so high, it is not easy to separate out spitefulness or revenge (on the part of either parent) from anything like a pure desire to care for one's children. When asked why they don't simply acquiesce to the system, letting their wives take custody, men typically say that they were considering the best interests of the children. A man from Ohio says, "Whenever you feel you're the better parent deep in your heart, you ultimately feel that, in the long run, the children will be better off—no matter what the short-term consequences, no matter what the price you have to pay."

But it is the nature of the custody process to lead men to define their desire to care for their children in legal terms—fitness, unfitness, best interests—rather than in terms of their emotional connectedness to their children, to their desire or need to love and be loved on a full-time basis. The same Ohio man, pressed a little, says, "Assuming we're both fit, why should I be the one to give up the children and be forced into the role of a nonparent, which is essentially the role you're in when you just have visitation rights? I would never buy it. If I had listened to friends who said, 'Just start a new life,' it might have been O.K. in the short run; but in the long run, how would I feel to

46

know that my relationship with my children was destroyed forever?"

CONFRONTING FATHERHOOD

There are no accurate national statistics on the number of men who have been awarded custody of their children.[23] Data from the United States Bureau of the Census indicates that between 1970 and 1974 the percentage of those children under six years of age living with a divorced father was increasing faster than the percentage of those children under six living with a divorced mother (37 percent compared to 31 percent); however, Dr. Paul Glick, senior census demographer, warns that the number of men shown as having custody of these children (48,000) is too small a percentage of the total population to be considered as solid statistical confirmation of a trend.[24] .

Nevertheless, experts in family law and counseling are quick to cite cases—contested and, increasingly, uncontested—where fathers have taken custody. A prominent New York attorney, for example, tells of a recent divorce in which her client, a woman with a flourishing career in the broadcasting industry, was more than willing to concede that her husband, a high-school teacher, could do the better job of raising their daughter, and to relieve his financial burden she agreed to pay a substantial amount of money in child support. George Williams, executive director of Parents Without Partners, estimates that the number of men gaining custody stands at almost 15 percent, up from the 10 percent reported in 1969 in Bernard Schlesinger's *One-Parent Family*.[25]

Guesswork aside, one thing is for sure: in a society that does not expect men to choose to take responsibility for the care of young children, the single father provokes a complex set of reactions. If he has won custody, he may stand to other men as a symbol of victory, offering a glimmer of evidence that the system can be equitable; the particulars of his case—the briefs filed, arguments used, tactics, and especially the judge's opinion—are likely to be seized upon by other fathers trying to obtain custody. Just as likely, he may be seen as a victim, as if obtaining the custody he sought could only have rendered him helpless. Suddenly, there are invitations to dinner, extended with kindness and with the underlying thought that a man alone just can't cope. Colleagues at the office, especially male colleagues, offer comments as to how they find it an inconceivable situation: "I could never do it alone," or "I admire your courage," or, more frequently, "Gee, that's a tough situation. You ought to get married."

Still, it is not unusual for the man with custody to be taken as a brave explorer of the new sex-role frontier. According to a man from New York City who won custody of his one-and-a-half-year-old son,

> Women, trendy women who are *into* the media or photography, come up to me and say, "I hear you're a single father. I think that's wonderful!" This glamorization of the role is often a result of political trends, fallout from the women's movement. It has nothing to do with me as a person. It's like coming up to a black musician and saying, "I've always admired black musicians. I think you people have such wonderful rhythm." You notice that nobody slaps a woman on the back for being a single mother. Nobody says, "Gee, that's really great, Dorothy;" it's just expected of Dorothy. Single-parent women shouldn't be taken for granted, and single-parent men shouldn't be slapped on the back for their courage.

A woman who lost custody of her daughter after a vicious family-court battle that dragged on for two and one half years agrees: "The fact that my ex-husband wanted to care for her is very beautiful. But it burns me up that he gets points for being the modern man of the seventies who's breaking down the sexist stereotypes, because when he had all the privileges of being a full-time working father, he took *all* the privileges. He refused to work out any arrangements for sharing child care—even on weekends." As much as she begrudges the image some people now confer on her ex-husband, though, she readily offers that it is one she is drawn to as she dates other men: "If you're a single woman and you meet a single father, a man who's fought for custody, you do tend to say '*Wow*'; you can't help wondering, because he wanted the kids, if he isn't all the things your ex-husband wasn't."

No matter how involved they have been with their children prior to divorce, the fact of single parenthood demands that men confront *all* the daily responsibilities of child rearing, all that must be done in everyday life just to cope, to find room for oneself and for one's child. For many men, becoming a single father does not mean living—as television shows like "The Courtship of Eddie's Father" suggest—in the sentimental glow of a deceased (and idealized) ex-wife and launching a campaign to find the children a new mother while the live-in help goes about the daily business of taking care of them; it means, instead, arriving at a new perspective on child care in our society and a new consciousness about themselves as parents.

The most immediate and persistent need of single fathers is, naturally, to find good day care for their children while they are at work. It is a need faced, of course, by single-parent mothers, but not in the same way. In a society that expects them to work outside the home, some men find that they have special privileges. For example, some day-care centers give preference to children of single fathers, implicitly assuming that men need or should be allowed to work more than do women.

But such sexism cuts two ways; it is not uncommon for men to encounter questions about why they, and not their wives, are looking for day care. A man from Manhattan's upper west side was about to have custody of his four-year-old son transferred—in a relatively amicable out-of-court settlement—from his ex-wife to himself. His ex-wife, who was now taking a job, would keep the child only until he found a day-care program. After visiting several centers, he noted a pattern of questioning: "Why do *you* have him? Why can't he be with his mother?" . . . "Do you really need us? If he can be with his mother for the next two weeks, why can't he be with her all the time?" . . . "Why can't he be with *your* mother?"

Finally he pulled what he refers to as the histrionic welfare routine: "I just started screaming, 'God damn it, if you don't give me day care, I'm going to write to the Governor and say I had to quit my job and go on welfare because you wouldn't give me day care!'"

His son was accepted, no more questions asked. However,

to this day, the announcements sent home from the day-care center are all addressed "Dear Mother," the envelopes even personalized to his wife. "If I were a woman, I wouldn't respond to that. I'd say I wasn't born Edward and I wasn't born Mrs. Thomas. This whole thing has really made me a feminist!"

The double standard applies even more pervasively, if in more subtle ways, at work. It is not unusual for an employer—especially a male employer—to meet the request of a female employee to leave the office a half hour early to pick up the kids, or take them to the doctor, and so forth. But men are not supposed to have such child-caring responsibilities, or any responsibilities that will divert them from the job. Single fathers frequently mention the implicit pressures they feel at work.

"It was an attitude," says an accountant for a large import-export firm. "People at my level didn't run out the door at five o'clock. It's not really that there was so much work to do. My boss was a man with a penchant for working long hours. I think he wanted me and everybody else to create the impression that we were killing ourselves the way he was. I could have maintained that job if I could have worked two or three nights a week until seven P.M. But there was no way I could do that. It was true that I was always running out the door at five; the day-care center wasn't too keen on parents who didn't pick their kids up at six."

Another man, formerly on the public relations staff of a petroleum company, speaks about the new perspective on his job that developed after he took custody of his four-year-old daughter: "I'd be sitting there at the end of the day in these meetings worrying if I was going to be able to get out in time to pick Stephanie up. Nothing we were talking about seemed as important to me as that. Luckily, I found a different job where they understand my situation a little bit better."

For single fathers who don't have jobs, the double standard can make itself felt through the welfare bureaucracy. Dick Chambers took custody of his daughter, Ericka, when she was two and a half years old; six months later he lost his job. Figuring that both he and Ericka would be better off if he stayed home, he applied for welfare.

"When Ericka was three, she was sick fairly often. It was

difficult to hold a job. Day-care centers don't take sick kids, and I really couldn't afford to keep hiring a baby-sitter. I've known of women who can't hold jobs because of kids, so they go on welfare. When I applied, I was told that if I couldn't find a job, they'd find me one for fifty dollars a week. A mother of a three-year-old would not be expected to work because the child needs the mother."

To balance his need for income with his need to be with his daughter when she was ill, he ended up taking work as a secretary-typist through a temporary employment agency. "The only thing I could have done, other than to take on typically female work, would have been to join a woman's consciousness-raising group where I could talk about the oppression of the male-dominated system. I never thought I'd say that, but my problems are the same as a woman's problems. What this society needs are services that help people find jobs that let them work and take care of their children."

Day care is a problem that single fathers—like single mothers—face, not only when they have to work, but if they want any type of social life apart from their children. Bill Malloy, a man from New York who took custody of his two-year-old son after his wife realized that she couldn't handle him, says, "I wanted Tommy all along, but my lawyer said there was no way. So, I visited on weekends and even two evenings a week. Still, my hours were pretty much my own. It wasn't uncommon for me to be out until one or two in the morning and then catch up on sleep after work the next day. But after we switched custody, I had to make sure that at eight P.M. I had a newspaper and cigarettes in the house. I wouldn't dare leave him alone, even for a minute; if he woke up to go to the bathroom and found me gone, he'd freak."

Baby-sitters are the obvious and most frequently used solution. However, many single fathers are sensitive about providing continuity for their children. "If you want to leave your kid with someone he's never seen before," says a man from Indiana, "it's possible to find lots of so-called qualified people. Maybe that's more my problem than his. I don't like to keep leaving him with strangers."

If they can afford it, single fathers hire housekeepers to

provide continuity. However, even with the money to pay for live-in help, there can be complications. A family therapist from California who gained custody of his four children reports "I got a lot of feedback from the women I interviewed about what the nature of my relationship would be with them. Half of them were afraid I was looking for a mistress; the other half were afraid I wasn't. It never occurred to me to get another man to help take care of them!"

To meet their own individual needs and the needs of their children, some single fathers *are* forging new solutions—finding single-parent roommates, male or female, or forming single-parent communes. After three months of being a single father, twenty-six-year-old Bill Malloy decided that he would do better by Tommy and himself if he were able to make parenting a shared arrangement. And he didn't mean a marriage arrangement.

"I wasn't about to get married for the sake of the child. I did that once and it was enough; but with the demands a child makes on you, I think it's difficult unless you can share. I didn't have to reject Tommy in order to avoid isolating myself. I just had to change the circumstances." He started going through the Roommate Wanted ads in New York's *Village Voice*, most of which, as it turned out, were placed by single-parent women who wanted to live with single-parent women. "I called one woman in Brooklyn, but she said she only wanted feminists. Later she called me back—she couldn't get any feminists to move in. I don't think she was really a feminist."

Malloy decided to run his own ad. "Single father and son looking for single parent with young child to share apartment. Shared responsibilities: baby-sitting, cooking, etc." Although the ad did not specify sex, all of the calls were from single-parent women. After meeting with several (and their children), Malloy and a woman named Alice—a thirty-two-year-old editor with a seven-year-old daughter named Jenny —decided that they would look for an apartment together. Though neither earned more than $12,000 a year, they were able, with their combined incomes, to find a spacious $450 apartment on Manhattan's upper west side, an apartment with far more running room for young children than either of them could afford individually.

"It worked out terrific for the kids, in every way. They got along great, and we met our mutual baby-sitting needs. My schedule was eight to three thirty, and I had to leave by seven A.M.; Alice's hours were ten to six. So she would handle the kids in the morning, get them dressed and off to school with bag lunches. I'd pick them up at four fifteen from a baby-sitter and make supper so we could all eat together when Alice got home. Then in the evening we adjusted our schedules according to who wanted to do what. Each of us knew there was somebody at home that the kids knew and liked. The kids said it was like a family."

The only people who had trouble accepting the arrangement were the women Bill dated and the men Alice dated. "We agreed on and had a nonsexual relationship, but we used to get the funniest reactions. When people came to the apartment for the first time, they tried to act very cool, very enlightened. But the women I started seeing regularly couldn't believe I wouldn't be sleeping with Alice. And Alice used to get the same thing thrown up at her too."

After two and a half years, when Alice remarried and moved out (she still visits frequently), Malloy again ran his roommate wanted ad in the *Village Voice*. This time he wanted to maintain the continuity of Tommy's life—his own room in the large apartment, his school, his friends in the neighborhood. After another careful screening process, Malloy found a new roommate—a forty-year-old single father with a daughter exactly Tommy's age. With the passing of an initial testing period by both children, the arrangement promises to be a good one; the kids are already calling one another sister and brother, and the adults are able to share in housekeeping, baby-sitting, and so on. Only one problem, totally unanticipated, has cropped up: When either of the two children call out "Daddy" in their indistinguishably high-pitched voices, both fathers come running!

Whatever new living arrangements single fathers make— with other single parents, baby-sitters, even with housekeepers

—the fullness of their responsibility to their children brings, more often than not, a new consciousness about parenthood. In a culture whose message to women is that they will have, should have, more responsibility or concern for the dailiness of their children's lives than their husbands, it is not unusual for men, no matter how involved they are with their children, to be involved in a different way.

"I was a passive parent," says one man who, during his marriage, followed the active decision-making lead of his wife regarding innumerable matters of household policy, some seemingly small (whether or not the children could have snacks, and what kind—between meals or after dinner), and some which seemed, to him, to have larger implications for the quality of their children's lives and minds—for example, what type of TV shows they could watch, or how long they could watch on a given day.

> I never liked the idea of them watching television, but they were watching it all the time—Saturday morning, Sunday morning, after school. Alan would come home from school, turn on the TV, and just sit there. They were lethargic, totally dead in front of the tube. She said they needed to relax. I said there were lots of ways to relax, but didn't make an issue of it. After all, I thought, it was her responsibility. But I was just being passive, not facing my responsibility. Now, with Ellen gone, there's nobody to defer to. Everything becomes a major experience; not only TV watching, but Christmas-time toys, the type of food they eat, the friends they play with. Every day I have to examine how *I* feel about these things, what I should do about them, what sort of people I want to help them become. I limit the TV now. We've talked about it, and the funny thing is that the kids don't really seem to mind. They've found plenty of other things to do.

Increased consciousness of the values they impart to their children does not come to single fathers without increased sensitivity to the logistics of child rearing. "What hit closest to me," says a man who now shares custody of two young girls, "is that, even though I was a good father, I wasn't a full parent, that I was only around in minor ways when it came to all the duties of taking care of them—arranging for doctors, dentists, and baby-sitters, noticing if they needed new shoes. None of these things are difficult in and of themselves. But it's the actual consciousness that these things have to be done that was foreign to me, and that can take on a never-ending burden."

For another man who fought for custody of his children and won, the daily responsibilities were largely unanticipated: "Most men don't appreciate the logistical problems of the suburban housewife. The problem of coordinating the laundry, chauffeuring, and food purchasing was a nightmare. It was the biggest shock of my life, especially because it interfered terribly with my relationship with the kids. We had screaming, raging, and crying until I broke down and pleaded helpless and realized that I didn't have to do everything. Now I pay lots more attention to what the five-year-old wants to do to help out."

This double discovery—that the responsibilities of parenthood are enormous *and* that children are capable of assuming far more responsibility than the fathers (or their ex-wives) ever thought or allowed—is a common one for single fathers. It is a discovery born of practical necessity after patterns of child rearing established in marriage break down.

"I give them a lot more *freedom* and *responsibility* now," says one single father, echoing almost verbatim the phrase used by many.

> Take clothes, for example. Barbara and I used to lay out the kids' clothes the night before, and Tammy would say, "I don't want to wear that." But after a fuss, she wore "that" because that's what Mommy and Daddy picked out for her. But I've realized, what do I care which pants or dress or top she wears? What's important is how she feels about herself, not what the outfit looks like. The end product is her being able to choose, knowing she *can* have some choice. All this came to me in the mornings when I'd be running like crazy to give the kids a good breakfast and get them to school on time. I was aggravating myself and them by feeling I had to do things for them. It was a pattern inherited from the marriage, and it affected all areas of my relationship with them. Like baths—

Barbara and I used to run to wash them and wipe them dry. But they're very capable of doing it themselves. Now they do it, and by the time I'm finished doing the dishes, they're into their pajamas.

Faced with more chores to do than before, some single fathers also realize—if they haven't before—that even young children can assume some household responsibility. "There are limits to what a four-year-old can do," says the father of children aged four and six. "You can't be a perfectionist, expecting everything to be done the way you'd like. But I just couldn't do it all my myself. I was getting grumpy at the kids because I felt overburdened with trying to get all our meals and laundry and everything else done. They realized that the house wasn't getting cleaned by magic and were glad to sit down and talk about what they could do to help. They're very excited and proud about helping to do the laundry. We fold it together on the playroom floor. Now, if they want to wear something, they know how it gets from the hamper and back into their drawer."

Another father with sons aged twelve, ten, and eight, says, "In order to have some time for myself, and in order to spend a better-quality time with them, I had to enlist more of their cooperation. Bruce vacuums on weekends, Richard and Todd clean the bathrooms, and they all help out during the week. I can't understand why we didn't share more before. The kids don't begrudge it; they understand that they're part of a team, part of a family."

Single fatherhood usually grows out of a crisis experience. If coping with the crisis induces men to figure out new ways to make a family function, it can also lead them to discover their children as persons and, in the process, to become fuller persons themselves.

A man who now shares custody with his ex-wife reports,

Before we split up, I spent time with the kids and I did all the things you're supposed to do, but I didn't have any connection with them as people, with who they were, what they wanted to become. My job was to be with them at certain times, to physically *be* with them—to take them downtown, to read them stories—that was part of the job. And I did a good job.

But now it's different. There are these two human beings I live with; they're not fully responsible to take care of themselves, but they're two people, very different people, with their own needs. To respond to these two human beings who are part of my life, it's not just a matter of filling some fatherhood role, saying, "Come on, kids, do this because Daddy says," but of trying to understand how they feel. The kids don't automatically tell me what they're feeling, not even when I ask how they feel about this or that, or when I say, "Let's talk." I find it works better if I tell them how I feel about something. Sometimes that's been hard for me. But I've opened up a lot. A lot of times I feel very proud of myself—for being sensitive to them, for really tuning in to their feelings. I'm connecting with my kids—when they're happy or when they really need help, when they're sad and need me in all kinds of emotional ways. And I'm connecting with myself.

To women who have lost custody in court, it often comes as a shock to find that their ex-husbands are confronting fatherhood and managing well; that despite the practical problems of day care and the logistics of housework, they are enjoying it; that they and the children have grown. Not that they want to get back with their ex-husbands, or vice versa. If they have been through a courtroom fight, most couples find the hostility fueled by the adversary system too great to allow for any reconciliation. Says one woman who now visits her four-year-old daughter every other weekend and four weeks during the summer, "Under different circumstances, I think we could have worked things out. We were adversaries when we began contending custody, and then we got forced into a system that made us even worse adversaries. This archaic system is poisonous."

TOWARD THE BEST INTERESTS—OF MEN, WOMEN, AND CHILDREN

If King Solomon were alive today, he would probably not want to be presiding in family court. Every year brings a substantial increase in the number of divorces, but little change in the procedures used to determine child custody. By March 1975, for example, when forty-five out of fifty states had adopted some form of no-fault divorce—which, in its purest form, produces the dissolution of a marriage upon the request of one spouse—almost all states maintained the adversary process for determining custody. So, whatever their wisdom, judges are increasingly put into the Solomon's dilemma of distilling the "best interests of the child" from courtroom scenarios in which the child's parents are hell-bent on proving each other unfit.

In the face of such unpleasant choices, the maternal presumption—whether stated explicitly by law or followed implicitly in practice—has been and continues to be a convenient formula. For a society in which everybody knew or was willing to accept a prescribed role, it may have worked well; Daddy could continue to be the sole breadwinner, Mommy to be the full-time homemaker and child rearer. But ours is a society in which traditional sex roles are in flux—in which, most significantly, some 40 percent of women with children under the age of eighteen are in the paid labor force, including 29 percent of those women with children under the age of three. And every year the figure is increasing.

The consequences of such changes are complex. On the one hand, they are bringing long overdue recognition that parenting and working outside the home are not mutually exclusive activities—for women *or* for men. On the other, they increasingly challenge the judiciary to consider how the best interests of children can be protected in a way that acknowledges the equal rights of both parents. In a society in which roles are in flux, custody decisions—which have always been among the most difficult to make ("Legal training and experience are of little practical help in solving the complex problems of human relations," admits one judge)—are becoming more difficult.[26] If a child's mother works and the father says that he is willing to quit work and stay home (as almost happened in one recent case), does that mean the child will be better off with the father? Isn't this a form of discrimination against working mothers? If a child's mother plans to remarry and continue staying at home, is the child necessarily better off with her? Isn't this a form of discrimination against working fathers? Is a remarried parent of either sex to be preferred over a single parent? Isn't this discrimination against the single-parent family? Given a case where there is no gross or obvious negligence on the part of one parent or the other, what is a judge to do? How can the "best interests of the child" be promoted?

According to Professors Joseph Goldstein, Anna Freud, and Albert J. Solnit, they can't. In a 1973 treatise entitled *Beyond the Best Interests of the Child*—perhaps the most significant and provocative recent contribution to the theory of state intervention in family affairs—they recommend that the best interest standard be superseded, that the "overall guideline for decision" should be "that placement which is least detrimental among available alternatives for the child":

> To use "detrimental" rather than "best interest" should . . . serve to remind decisionmakers that their task is to salvage as much as possible out of an unsatisfactory situation. It should reduce the likelihood of their becoming enmeshed in the hope and magic associated with "best," which often mistakenly leads them into believing that they have greater power for doing "good" than "bad." [27]

There is more than a semantic distinction here. Under the standards proposed by Goldstein, Freud, and Solnit, "Each child placement would be treated as a matter of urgency to be finally resolved in days, not years." [28] There would be no long-drawn-out court proceedings, but a "quick, final, and unconditional disposition to either of the competing parents." [29]

How would the decision be made? According to these psychoanalytically disposed scholars, placement should be with the child's "psychological parent," i.e., the one parent with whom the child has the most continuous daily interaction, for "disruptions of continuity" in the care of infants and young children can induce severe physical reactions and psychological distress that may hinder the development of all future attachments. ("Such reactions occur even if the infant's care is divided merely between mother and babysitter.") [30]

In the case of two equally acceptable "psychological parents," Goldstein, Freud, and Solnit note that "a judicially supervised drawing of lots . . . might be the most rational and least offensive process for resolving the hard choice." [31] But given current child-rearing practices, their guidelines would mean that, in most cases, women would become exclusive custodial parents because, in most cases, women are the primary caretakers of young children.

Whether or not such guidelines would really go "beyond" the best interests of the child *or* meet the best interests of women is highly debatable. As feminist literature has made abundantly clear, many women have become primary caretakers not just because they are capable and devoted to their children, but because they have grown up in a society that conditions them to be mothers while offering them few other alternatives. To respond to the best interests of both children and women, argue Susan Gettleman and Janet Markowitz—psychotherapists and coauthors of the widely acclaimed *The Courage to Divorce*—it would be socially advantageous to make it the normal practice to award custody to fathers. By relinquishing formal custody to their husbands, women would be in a better position to "devote more time and energy to education and job training and can move more rapidly toward economic self-sufficiency."

> It seems to us [say Gettleman and Markowitz] that a father with a good income could hire a competent housekeeper during the day. (The children could then have the male *and* female "identification models" the experts claim they need at home.) On the other hand, a woman cannot readily "hire" a man to stay home with her children while she goes out to work. Fathers with custody would see their children often, but the children would not simultaneously be deprived of female attention, since they see women all the time in nurseries, schools, and playgrounds. As long as isolated nuclear families are *the* mode of rearing children, it makes more sense to urge fathers to take custody.[32]

While mindful of the very real economic imbalances in our society, the Gettleman and Markowitz proposal offers no more of a just solution to custody adjudication than does the maternal presumption. It highlights, instead, just how difficult it is—when a marriage breaks down—to respect the well-being of two parents and their children.

While there are no formulas, attempts are being made by

some divorced couples to recognize the best interest of children as well as the rights and responsibilities of both parents. At the end of a marriage, some men and women are working out a new solution—equally shared custody and care of their children—that provides a glimmer of movement beyond both sex-based presumptions and courtroom acrimony.

For Ted and Jeannette Lewis and their two children—seven-year-old Richard and four-year-old Cynthia—it works like this. Jeannette moved out of the apartment in Brooklyn and set up house a half mile away. She takes care of the children from after school on Wednesday until Saturday at 5:00 or 6:00 P.M., when she brings them to Ted or has him pick them up. Ted takes care of them from Saturday evening until Wednesday morning, when he takes them to school. The arrangement gives each parent a weekend night free and a weekend day to share with the kids. On weekdays, whoever takes the children to school has responsibility for them during the day. The children have the same school, the same friends, and both parents—separately, but equally.

The arrangement worked out by the Lewis family provided the model for another couple getting ready to go through the agony of a divorce. According to Sam Brown, "I didn't know what I was going to do. I knew I didn't want to lose contact with the children. I didn't want visitation rights, but I knew I didn't stand a chance of getting full custody in court. And full custody isn't what I wanted either. Neither Judy nor I were feeling terribly fond of one another, but we knew the kids loved both of us and we loved the kids. I'm not sure what would have happened if I hadn't heard about the Lewises, or if Judy hadn't thought it was a good idea." Any family that opts for sharing custody in this way has to tailor arrangements to its own particular needs and, optimally, with some flexibility. The Browns have a schedule which alternates the weekend days because Judy didn't want to be stuck with all Sundays, when lots of places she wanted to take the children were closed.

Several other families share the care in much the same way, with the important distinction that it is the parents, not the children, who switch from one home to another. It is a more expensive arrangement because it requires maintenance of the original house or apartment for the children as well as two separate living spaces—usually less elegant, to say the least—for the parents. But the compromise by the adults on their living quarters allows the children to maintain one unchanging place that is always their own.

The concept of shared custody flies in the face of traditional psychiatric and legal opinion. Splitting custody usually conjures the image of splitting a child in two, if not physically, as King Solomon once proposed, then mentally; given the insecurity of a divorce, a child should at least know which parent is the real parent, which home the real home. But opinion is changing, partly through recognition that the father's role in child development has been undervalued. Clinical psychologist Henry Biller, coauthor of *Father Power*, recommends that two homes can be better than one:

> The whole concept of custody can be both psychologically unsound and much too rigid to fit all individual cases. Since fathers and mothers are both important to a child's development, it should be assumed from the start that each parent is equally entitled to aid in raising the child. . . . The custody method of awarding child-care rights can be extremely difficult for the child. In effect, he may be asked to choose one parent *or* the other. On the other hand, by abandoning a rigid custody concept, the child's security may be boosted at a time when he badly needs it.[33]

While the shared-care arrangement represents one promising alternative for adults and children, it has, at best, limited application. With every year, the number of divorces increases. And in most cases parents are going to court because, for whatever reasons, they cannot see their way clear to *any* type of sharing. The custody concept, then, is no more likely to disappear than is divorce.

However, a variety of reforms are being suggested—or tried out—that might help reduce both the adversary element and sex bias from custody determination. Diana Dubroff, a New York matrimonial lawyer, is spearheading the implementation, on a private trial basis, of a Humanized Divorce Service—

a panel of experts (psychiatrists, psychologists, appropriately trained lawyers) who, without the presence of attorneys advocating one side or the other, would hear all information relevant to a family dispute (presented by parents, children, relatives, etc.) and make a *nonbinding* recommendation to both parents.[34] Meanwhile, family counselors are developing a new specialty, divorce counseling, the goal of which is not to help a husband and wife "solve their problem" or achieve a reconciliation, but to guide them—in an impartial and supportive atmosphere—through some of the practical decisions such as child care and custody that have to be made when a marriage breaks down.

In his capacity as adviser to the American Bar Association, child psychologist Lee Salk (who won custody of his own children in 1975 in a precedent-setting New York case; neither Dr. Salk nor his wife claimed the other to be unfit as a parent) is stressing to lawyers and judges the importance of listening to and respecting the preference of the child, even the young child. Such a policy has been adopted in New Jersey, where the 1974 legislature approved a bill granting to a child who is mature enough "to form intelligent preference as to custody" the right to express that preference.[35] To further enhance respect for the rights of the child, legal scholars Henry Foster, Jr., and Doris Jonas Freed are urging the mandatory appointment, in all cases, of a separate attorney to represent the child's interests.[36]

Perhaps the most radical proposal for reform—divorce insurance—deals only indirectly with custody, but has enormous potential for affecting its determination. When Diana Dubroff introduced the concept of divorce insurance in 1971, it seemed like an impossible idea; but every year, as it becomes more clear that divorce is one of the normal hazards of contemporary life, it is being taken more seriously. Theoretically, annual premium payments somewhat comparable to those now paid for life insurance would guarantee a couple that, at the time of divorce, a sum of money would be available to be used for child rearing. By relieving to some extent the financial pressures experienced by women with little or no earning power and by men who find themselves facing the support of two homes, divorce insurance would facilitate more equitable and rational solutions to custody determinations.

Dr. Carolyn Shaw Bell, professor of economics at Wellesley College, goes one step further, advocating not optional divorce insurance but "compulsory child-care insurance to which parents would contribute equally." [37] Child-care insurance would protect children against the ever-increasing possibility of their parents' divorce and would "specifically separate the functions of childbearing from child rearing," allowing child care to become more readily "an economically viable occupation, perhaps for one or the other parent—regardless of sex." [38]

With or without divorce insurance, attorneys for children, or the help of psychiatric experts, judges will still have to deduce, from a complicated and delicate network of fact and feeling, the best interests—or, as recently suggested, the "least detrimental" alternative—for the child. The extent to which the law or the courts will be able to facilitate change that respects the best interests of each child and the equal rights of both parents is unpredictable. As legal scholar Michael Wheeler says, "Because the controversy about child custody strikes so many emotional chords, the issue is usually tabled when family laws are revised. Compromise seems to lead back to the status quo, not out of any affection for the present system, but out of a feeling that reform of divorce laws should not be jeopardized by disagreement about what should be done about custody." [39]

For example, California, which in 1970 became the first state to eliminate fault completely as a grounds for divorce, left its custody laws almost intact; custody in California now goes to either parent according to the child's best interests, "but, other things being equal, custody shall be given to the mother if the child is of tender years." [40]

A major impetus for change could come either from passage of the Equal Rights Amendment to the Constitution, which would prohibit any presumptions about custody based on the sex of the parent, or from a Supreme Court decision. But the Court has yet to hear a case that confronts the denial of custody to a father because of sex bias. In 1973, it dismissed an appeal from the California ruling in favor of mothers, and in 1974 it declined to hear David Arends' appeal that the Utah Supreme Court's endorsement of the maternal presumption violated his constitutional rights.

What effect would a Supreme Court decision that the maternal presumption is unconstitutional have on custody awards? According to Rena K. Uviller, one of the attorneys from the American Civil Liberties Union who petitioned the Supreme Court on behalf of David and Kimberly Arends:

> Whether new laws or opinions create social change or vice versa is a very complex issue. But I think the question of men getting custody is going to follow and not initiate social change; that men will get custody when women have better pay and status, and when we have flexible working hours that allow and encourage men and women to participate equally in the care of their children. Of course, a Supreme Court decision would have significant effects. It would have forced lower courts to look at custody cases more closely, to examine how they're making their awards, if they're really considering evidence about how many hours a man spends with his child, what the nature of each parent's work is, which parent seems more psychologically or temperamentally suited to taking care of the children, what the quality of the relationship is, and what really is in the best interests of the child. Judges are supposed to be doing this now, but they don't always. A Supreme Court decision would make judges more wary because of possible appeals on grounds of sex bias. It would also encourage more men to seek custody who don't even try now; they're told it's impossible.

3

MAKING THE TIME TO CARE:
PART-TIME JOBS
FOR FULL-TIME FATHERS

"If Madame Curie were alive today and only able to work from 9:30 to 3:15, would you hire her?"

So goes the motto of Newtime, Inc., a New York City employment agency founded in 1970 by two women who have been selling a revolutionary idea: the twenty-five hour work-week. Newtime's rationale is that there are millions of talented women who want to work—but who are not in the job market for one simple reason: the traditional nine-to-five job is out of sync with their child-caring needs. By breaking the tradition, by making working time more compatible with family time, the business community can vastly increase its pool of talented and highly motivated potential employees, and American mothers can lead more balanced lives.

Newtime is not alone in its efforts. In 1962 five college presidents founded Catalyst "to stem the conspicuous waste of training and ability among many of the 14 million college-educated women in the U.S."; ever since, Catalyst has been promoting part-time job options and counseling women who are trying to reconcile work and "family obligations." In 1967 Washington Opportunities for Women began functioning two days a week—with a volunteer staff of two—to develop professional part-time jobs for women. In its first year, the agency helped 500 women and was in touch with 250 employers; in 1974 it had grown to include twenty-two paid staff (full- and part-time), thirty-five regular volunteer counselors, six other counseling centers in East Coast cities and had been in touch with over 10,000 women and 1500 employers. In 1972 a Chicago-based outfit, Flexible Careers, began trying to convince employers that the nine-to-five schedule deprived them of a "fresh pool of skilled workers, primarily women."

Some employers, while not setting out to hire Madame Curie, have responded to the needs of the female labor force. In a September 24, 1974, editorial entitled "The Family and the Firm," *The Wall Street Journal* said, "We are intrigued with a small experiment being conducted by Honeywell, Inc., in Massachusetts on behalf of working mothers . . . the mothers are being offered short work shifts that fall within school hours. Thus, they are able to give full attention to their children and earn an income as well." [1] The *Journal* went on to praise this creative scheduling as a sign of the corporate responsibility necessary to prevent the disintegration of the American family, a disintegration clearly related to the increase in working mothers.

The logic behind the *Journal's* editorial—and behind most of the agencies advocating part-time opportunities—holds women to be the mainstay of family life; if more women want to work, then society has a responsibility to help alleviate the conflict between the demands of work and of child-care responsibilities. In one sense, it is a logic in recognition of and in service to increased opportunities for women. In another, however, it highlights the extent to which our society avoids any examination of the relationship between work by men and family life. No agenices were established specifically to counsel men who wanted part-time work so that they could maintain their family obligations, or to advise businesses on how they could accommodate and profit from part-time male employees. *The*

Wall Street Journal found no occasion to praise Honeywell or any other company because of its enlightened policies for working fathers. Even the Bureau of Census, which classified part-year employees according to what they do during most of the weeks in which they didn't work, restricted the "taking care of family or home" category to women.[2]

To accept women into the labor force is one thing. To create or even to conceive of conditions that might allow or encourage men to reduce their working hours and increase their participation in child rearing is quite another. It is, for the most part, incomprehensible to the business community. Ina Torton of Newtime, Inc., says:

There's a stigma attached to a man who wants part-time work. It means he's not masculine, not aggressive. The attitude of society toward a man not gung-ho on his career is even less kind than that toward women who want part-time work. He's got a double hurdle. He's not only stuck in the low-end jobs, but even the low-end jobs don't want him because they don't understand why he wants to be there. Regarding women, at least society understands that she's got a conflict between career and children; women are supposed to be in conflict. A man—it's expected he has someone else taking care of his children for him. A man who wants part-time work has the reverse problem of a career woman—for her, it's always "Who's taking care of your children?" For him, it's "Why do you want to?"

Newtime once received a request from a small law firm in New York City that wanted to hire someone with general corporate experience on a part-time basis. The agency referred a man in his late twenties, a graduate of New York University Law School with a good academic and work record. He wanted part-time work and went for three interviews with the prospective employer, but finally didn't get the job.

"His qualifications were fine," says Ina Torton. "They just couldn't feel comfortable with a man who wanted part-time work. They didn't realize when they advertised a part-time position that they really meant to hire a woman."

The stigma about men working part time—unless at a second job—was confronted dramatically by Share Employment,

Inc., a Denver, Colorado, agency attempting since 1973 to secure part-time professional positions for women who want to work and maintain family life *and* for husbands and wives who want to share work and child care. The agency has been successful in placing women but not men, even though several couples have applied for part-time work. According to Gloria Golbert, codirector of Share Employment, most personnel managers frown (literally) at the mention of couples sharing jobs or men rearing children; when Ms. Golbert and her colleague appeared on a local TV program, they were introduced as "two crazy women from the East who are bringing a crazy radical idea to Denver."

Some indication of why the prospect of men increasing their child-rearing time threatens the business community was revealed in April 1974 at public hearings of the California Fair Employment Practice Commission, the agency charged with preparing statewide guidelines for the elimination of sex discrimination in hiring practices. When several men and women asked the FEPC to recommend paternity leave as an option equivalent to maternity leave, one of the commissioners expressed strong objections. There was no public transcript of the hearings, but this commissioner—who asked that his name be withheld from publication—was very forthright in summarizing his commentary by telephone:

Small business cannot bear the brunt of all this childbearing deal. It may sound far-fetched to you, but I deal with the problems of the small businessman every day. Why should a businessman pay for a father to stay home? I think this women's lib stuff is fine, and I've argued for it all my life. But for a father to get leave is completely ridiculous. I've been a father and grandfather, and I don't see why a father should have to have leave. It doesn't make sense to me.

No man is really capable—fit physically or psychologically or by training—to take care of children. When my grandchildren are left at my home, if something goes wrong, I just can't cope—I fly all to pieces. I know you hear about these things today, but it's probably no more than one in a thousand when it works out.

A father can't take care of a child. He can't nurse a child.

Sure, he can learn, but say he's a skilled mechanic or an engineer. He takes off and the mother, who probably doesn't have the same level of skills, goes to work somewhere. He can cripple a small business. Even a good salesman in a small business—you take him away, and you can destroy the business.

I know the philosophy of all this, but it can go to extremes and endanger the whole economy. . . . I know a lot of these things aren't so politically good to be saying. I'm an honest ordinary businessman with a certain amount of sense about how things work.

From the proposed practice of allowing men to stay home without pay during the early infancy of their children, this public official envisioned the failure of small businesses (like the one he owned) and, consequently, of the whole economy; after all, if male (hence, skilled) labor withdrew, it would be replaced by relatively unskilled female labor. While the opinions of one of its members are not directly attributable to the commission as a body, they reveal, in this case quite dramatically, how personally held sexist attitudes and assumptions about male and female child-rearing roles might influence public policy. In its November 1974 guidelines for eliminating sex discrimination in hiring, the Fair Employment Practice Commission did not include paternity leave.

It is hardly realistic to think that, given the opportunity for paternity leave, men will withdraw en masse from the labor force. Both our social conditioning and the current differential in pay between jobs available to men and women preclude that. Of course, there are, as we shall see in Chapter 5, some men staying home full time to care for their children while their wives go to work outside the home; and more men with conventional jobs are challenging the stereotype of the father who comes home and hides behind the newspaper to minimize contact with his children. Still, the trend is not for men to reduce work, but for women to move—or try to move—into full-time jobs.

There are, however, some men who work part time because they feel they have something to lose unless involved in a more intimate and routine way in their children's early years than full-time jobs allow. Unlike homemaker-fathers, they don't

70

want to give up or suspend their careers, but they are unwilling to put career ahead of family. However convinced they are that quality of time spent with a child is more important than quantity, they also believe that quality *and* quantity are better than just quality. As one man says, "You put burdens on maintaining the quality the more the time is decreased. The reason you can't be intimate with a lot of other people is that you're not present long enough for the interaction and trust to develop; with a small child, it's especially important that he knows there's a continuing source there." These men are working part time—as are their wives—to establish balanced lives and intimacy with their children.

Because most jobs in America don't accommodate the needs of men to be with their children, it is, in effect, easier to work full time or stay home full time than it is to find good part-time work. As one woman who shares a college teaching position with her husband says, "It would be difficult for either of us to take a low-status part-time job. I don't know what we'd do; work alternate years maybe." An on-a-year-off-a-year pattern, even if possible, would provide little if any job continuity; and most people, men *or* women, don't want to be home full time. But the lives of those men who are working part time to share child care reveal the truth of a commonplace—that the structure of working time has an enormously powerful influence over our lives—and illustrate a vision—that changes in work structure are possible, and may open up important opportunities for men, women, and children.

PART-TIME CORPORATE EXECUTIVE

When Eric Barrett, the Assistant Director of Design and Implementation for Educational Systems Analysts (a pseudonym for the educational division of a large national corporation) asked about reducing his work week from five days to three, his boss was sure there was something wrong.

"Look, I want you to really tell me if you're looking for a way out," was the first thing the boss said.

Or, as Eric's wife, Pam, explains, "They were scared shitless that he'd leave."

Eric was the type of employee destined for success anywhere. He had been on the same trajectory all his life: straight As in high school, Phi Beta Kappa at Yale, and graduate work at the Harvard Graduate School of Education. He was hard-working, even driven, the model of a man who commits himself wholeheartedly to his work. At the age of thirty-one, after three and a half years at ESA, he was earning over $20,000. He was, you might say, the employee least likely to ask for part-time work; and that's what makes his example so significant. Like many similarly talented men working for corporations throughout the United States, he was just the employee most likely to have his request met. In fact, Eric didn't want to leave ESA, but he did want to spend more time with his four-months-old son, Tony.

No one would have guessed that by looking at Eric's life during Pam's pregnancy or even after Tony's birth. Eric was bearing down at work, removing himself more and more from the life Pam was leading in their Los Angeles home. They were drifting apart, and with the birth of their son, things got worse. Eric was up and off to work by the time Pam got up in the morning; her days were filled with Tony's needs, shopping, and work on quilts and other artsy-craftsy items for the house. By five o'clock, Pam was starving for adult company and at the same time hating herself for having to demand and need that from Eric.

When he got home, usually not before seven, they went through all the motions—"Hi" . . . "How are you?" . . . "How are *you?*" . . . "How was your day at work?" . . . "How's the baby?"—none of which helped Pam feel less lonely or Eric less excluded from the relationship Pam had with Tony. With communication breaking down, Pam would often go to sleep early, nursing Tony, her physical holding needs now met by her infant son, not her husband.

Just how far apart they had drifted became dramatically clear when Pam took four-months-old Tony home to her parents' house for a visit and found on her return that Eric had slept with several other women.

"It was as if something woke me up and showed me how dependent I was on Eric," says Pam. "It was frightening. I wasn't about to start pleading either." Her strongest impulse was to pull away from any more dependence on Eric. "I said, 'Fuck you, God damn it; I'm going to get my shit together.'"

More and more women are coming to this sort of awareness, if not for the same reason, then at least with the same anger as Pam, and with the same prospective solution: the part-time job. Get out of the house, earn some money, feel more self-esteem, pull one's own economic weight. Pam had been trained as a commercial artist at the Parson's School of Design and, before her marriage, had done some teaching and commercial art; she began to put a portfolio together.

When they joined a couples group, Eric found women members telling him how hard they would find it to be married to him; he was always pushing, he always wanted more. The very drive that made him so successful in business made him hard to be with at times; he expected too much from himself and too much from others. Eric started to express his feelings, too. He felt as limited in his role as Pam felt in hers. The dynamic worked both ways; if she was angry at her dependence, he was resentful about making all the money. And he felt very much left out—even pushed out—of fatherhood, as if Tony was Pam's child exclusively.

If the dynamic worked both ways, so did the solution. Somewhat to Pam's surprise, Eric said he was going to ask his boss if he could cut back to three days a week; anything less would have made him ineligible for life insurance, health insurance, and other benefits.

"It sort of all grew out of my wanting to change myself, the way I am. Also, I wanted to be with Tony. I didn't want him to have the same thing I had with my father. He was always off on business trips when I grew up. I really wanted to have some part in raising Tony. I grew up in a classic American home where the father makes all the money and makes all the decisions, and gets all the deference. I was just doing the same thing my father did. I get into this big-daddy thing, too, where I take all the responsibility for everything. I'd been aware of it before, but right then it seemed isolating to me. I wanted to open up, to loosen up."

To keep themselves from too easily drifting into old patterns, Eric and Pam agreed on an informal contractual relationship. He would take over two fifths of the child care and household duties and would be responsible for meeting three fifths of the basic living expenses. Pam, who was already starting to get jobs, would be responsible for two fifths of the expenses and three fifths of the child care. Weekends would be shared fifty-fifty.

"I was the catalyst," says Pam, "but he really wanted to change. I think he was scared. Not to keep driving yourself and earning money when that's what you've been taught to do all your life is a scary thing to start doing. It was hard for him to relax, and it was hard for me to change, to go out with a portfolio and take myself seriously, to experience failure and the possibility of being rejected. We each started doing a little of what the other was doing."

The contractual arrangement, including separate checking accounts for payment of the bills, has been abandoned, but at first it was a necessary and healthy thing to do.

"I needed that to know I was pulling my own weight financially," claims Pam. "I had a lot of money hang-ups anyway. My father would hand me a twenty-dollar bill and say, 'You've got to work for everything you get.'"

"A whole lot of good feelings got liberated by having this arrangement agreed to, deliberately calculated," Eric says.

> I don't feel that a lot of men ever have a chance to get into their feelings about their kid. Once I had a chance to get my hands in there, a whole lot of feelings started to come alive. I had cared about Tony, but it wasn't real personal and intimate. Once I started to spend time, I started to really love him and care about him a lot. Before, it was more of an intellectual relationship: I'm the father, that's my son. I got a lot more tender feelings. Being with him has opened up a side of me that I have trouble expressing otherwise. I had that whole macho thing about how men are supposed to be tough. I started talking to my own father about how hard he was to communicate with and how I'd like to change that, how we never really had any personal communication at all. In the process of doing that, he told me a lot about his own childhood. I hadn't really had any person-to-person communication with my father since I was in junior high school.

Since the age of seven months, Tony has had a lot of communication with his father. On the two weekdays when Eric is home (Eric and Pam say "That's a nice day"), everyone gets up at the same time. Eric makes breakfast and then, when Pam retires to her office in the house to design a parent-education brochure for a local school district, Eric gives his son, now age two, a morning bath. Tony "helps" Eric clean up the kitchen and the rest of the house, and then, on most days, they go out to play or work together in the yard. Tony has his own watering can and box of garden tools to help care for the vegetables and flowers; he even has a miniature wheelbarrow that he fills with small rocks to help Eric construct a stone wall across the front of the property. Often Eric, Pam, and Tony lunch together; but Pam's quitting time depends on how involved she is with a particular project. On occasion, she has heard from Eric the same objections she used to level at him about overinvolvement with work.

On days when Eric is working, Pam doesn't feel she's sitting around waiting for him to come home. She does her art work when Tony is napping, playing by himself in the fenced-in yard, or attending his now three-mornings-a-week play group. Because Eric is so fully involved with Tony, the evenings at home now mean, according to Pam, "not my dealing with Tony, then with Eric; it's the three of us dealing with one another." Having more time together has also meant that Eric and Pam feel comfortable taking time to develop as individuals, not just as a couple. Eric has taken up bass fiddle and plays folk music informally with a group of friends. Pam goes visiting or to movies:

"It's nice to feel free to go out one or two nights without your kid or your husband," she says, "to make friends outside of being friends as a couple."

It is not just relations with family that have eased up for Eric. Most of the people working with him have told him that he's a lot more human, more real, since he's started balancing his commitments to work and to child care. And it's not just because he's around the office less. It's that his attitude to others isn't as demanding and controlling. Although he hasn't relinquished his authority, he has eased up on having to be *the boss.*

"I consciously pulled back from that," he says. "As soon as I relinquished some of my time, other people moved in. I watched other people who had been there less time move in and do jobs I had been doing. That was tough. Sometimes I got jealous of people making decisions where I had before, but I quickly realized that it's not necessary to consolidate power in one person at the top. It really was an exercise in changing a pattern that wasn't working."

Eric claims, "If you want to share in the child care as I'm doing, you won't be president of the company."

On the other hand, ESA feels it's getting a good deal. Eric is so dynamic that his presence is still strongly felt. Of course, other people have had to take on tasks that Eric could have done better, and decisions have to be made without waiting for him. But while Eric was no slouch before, his immediate supervisor says, "Eric comes in so fresh and full every day that, on a daily basis, we get more input from him. When people work a five-day week, they're bound to have a weak day here and there; it's very seldom that any of Eric's three days is weak."

The arrangement Eric and Pam have made is one they plan to keep while Tony is young. Pam may start working three days a week; she is starting to get more work and could make up for the reduction in family income that resulted when Eric cut back and she started free-lancing. But she wouldn't take full-time work while Tony is young, "unless we were starving to death. I like being with him too much. And there's a really nice kind of family feeling from all this that I didn't expect. I don't know how to describe it."

As for Eric, he too plans to keep working part time while Tony is a preschooler. "I just don't think I could have the sort of relationship with him that I do unless I put in the time."

THE SMALL BUSINESS

Steve and Debby Hoffman, aged twenty-seven and twenty-six, are coowners and operators of Gold Star Publications, Inc., a printing business located in downtown Manhattan. They don't actually run printing presses, though for two years they did; two Multilith machines now stand idle at the back of the large room they occupy in a former warehouse. The Hoffmans provide consultation about layout, paper, typeface, or anything else related to printing. At any one time, they are busy shepherding forty to fifty jobs from the initial design stages through production: invitations to an ACLU benefit or an artist's cocktail party, the weekly newspaper for Pratt Institute, posters for the La Mama Theatre, mailers for Columbia University, even business cards. It is a young, promising business in what Debby Hoffman calls the "printingest city in the world."

The Hoffmans share their work and they share the care of their two-year-old son, Michael. At 8:00 A.M. on Monday, for example, Steve opens the shop. Debby stays home until nine, when she takes Michael downstairs to morning play group in their Brooklyn apartment building. Then Debby takes the subway to Manhattan to join Steve at the office. At noon, Steve leaves to pick Michael up from play group and spends the rest of the day with him. Debby comes home at 5:30 or 6:00 P.M. The next day, the pattern is reversed: Debby opens the shop at 8:00 A.M., works four hours, then spends the rest of the day with Michael; Steve takes Michael to play group and then works seven or eight hours at the shop. The schedule has varied with Michael's age and with the availability of babysitters, but it is a schedule of part-time work (twenty-five to thirty hours each per week) and sharing that the Hoffmans have maintained, more or less, ever since their son's birth.

It is also one that many people find hard to understand. The printing world is predominantly male. For Debby Hoffman, to be in a printing shop is odd enough; it is even more startling when printers and jobbers find out that if Debby is in the shop, it means that Steve is at home taking care of the baby. A fifty-year-old trade printer named Pete, who does a good deal of work for the Hoffmans, always asks when Debby picks up the phone, "Is Steve there?"

"No," says Debby.

"Where is he?"

"Pete," Debby pleads, "why do you want to torture your-self? You know what I'm going to say. He's home with the baby."

"He's home with the *baby?*"

To Pete, as to most people, it is incomprehensible. "What do you do with the baby?" he asks Steve continually. Just as continually he hears the reply, said with a broad grin of satisfaction, "I play."

Steve's mother wasn't sure what he would or might do with the baby either. Every day during Michael's early months she would call when it was Steve's turn for child care and say, "Did you feed him?" Steve's father wasn't worried that the baby would starve, but that the business would fold. He kept saying, "You really gotta get serious. You should work full time."

But working full time is exactly what neither Steve nor Debby wants to do. They could, to be sure. The work is there. They could build more accounts, start employing more people than their two half-day messengers and their part-time book-keeper. They could probably earn more than the $17,000 per year that they take home, roughly, between them, either by stepping up their business or by going out to get jobs with any of the top printing companies; they are highly skilled and could earn $20,000 each, starting salary. But to do so would mean working long days for somebody else, and it would mean a lot less time getting to know Michael.

The Hoffmans planned to share in Michael's care long before he was born. Equal responsibility for work and children was a premise of their marriage and, in large part, an out-growth of their involvement in the radical movement during and after college.

"I knew we were going to do it that way and no other," says Debby. "It was a matter of principle. We didn't have the details figured out, but I knew we'd figure them out."

Steve agreed, intellectually; emotionally, he wasn't so sure. Debby kept telling him, "You're really gonna love it," and he would say, "I don't know. What if he drives me crazy?" His anxiety level was as high as his ideological commitment; his politics told him this was the "right" way to do it, but it was hard to ignore twenty-five years of living in a society which taught men to have little if any relationship with young children.

By the time Michael was six months old, Steve was propelled home after a half day's work not by Debby's push or by any abstract sense of justice, but by Michael. "You don't need a lot to pull you toward him. When either Debby or I would come home from work, we'd burst out, 'What'd he do today?' He was a wonder, just a wonder. I could stare and look at him for hours. Here was this thing changing and growing. Every now and then I'd think, My God, you created him; he wouldn't have existed if it weren't for you two!"

Steve's desire to be with Michael transformed the very nature of the Hoffmans' printing business. Debby had been trying to convince Steve for a year before Michael's birth that they weren't making any profit from the Multilith presses and would fare better by shutting them down. They were wasting time on work they could easily job out; freedom from the machines would allow them to earn more by selling their expertise in design and production management. But Steve was stubborn; his father was a pressman, and he took pride at carrying on the family trade—and, he admits sheepishly, he simply liked playing with the machines.

However, as he began getting to know his infant son, Steve mellowed. "I wanted to spend time with him, and it was impossible to make up on the presses for the time that went to him. There was a limit to telling customers we don't print until Thursday because that's when I wouldn't be taking care of Mike!"

On his afternoons with two-year-old Michael, Steve does exactly what he told the disgruntled pressman, Pete: he plays—hide and seek, animal pretend, and word games prompted by what seems like an endless series of books.

"The baby kangaroo climbed into the————," reads Steve.

"Couch," grins Michael.

"Pouch," exclaims Steve, turning out his pants pockets, which they proceed to explore for the next five minutes. Their dialogue back and forth is continual and may explain in part why Michael is so verbal.

After Michael's two-hour nap, Steve usually takes him out —to the playground, on errands, to neighbors, anywhere to keep from feeling cooped up in the Hoffmans' small two-bed-room apartment. Steve even takes his son with him on business.

"They have statues of lions all over Columbia, because that's the school symbol or mascot. In one office, I go in to discuss a four-thousand-dollar printing job, and this high-level administrator just takes down one of the small lion statues so that Michael can play with it on the floor. We try to deal with clients who can relate to our life-style!"

There are limits, of course, to taking Michael along on the job and, despite what Steve says to Pete, of playing with him. Especially during Michael's infancy, Steve's sense of wonder was mixed with a terrible sense of isolation.

> I found myself just wanting to talk to an adult. Sometimes when Debby would come home, I'd say, "Talk to me, you never talk to me anymore. You go to work all day, you never talk." It was really crazy. A weird thing about being a man taking care of a kid is that there aren't any men taking care of kids. You go to the park and there's a lot of ladies around. I felt separate, really lonely. I met a guy who's an import-export trader for one of the big mineral trading companies. He was visiting Nancy across the street, and when I started asking him about his work, you could see that he just could have talked for years; he was really into it. That was O.K. with me, because I'm interested in that too, and you don't get many chances to speak with someone who does that type of big trading every day of his life. I really wanted to talk to him, but it never occurred to me to invite him over for a cup of coffee. If I were a woman and he were a woman, I would have invited him over for coffee in a minute. But, because I'm a man, I didn't think to relate on those terms.

Initially, there were difficulties at work, too. A client who called in the morning and dealt with Steve would call back in the afternoon and have to deal with Debby because Steve was at home with Michael. Or a printer getting ready to set type on a rush order that Debby had specked would call to find only Steve at the shop. Communication between the Hoff-mans on every detail of their work had to be complete and accurate; they had to be able to stand in for each other with their clients as easily as they did with their son. At first, this required frequent and frantic phone calls from the shop to the apartment, where one would demand of the other, "What the hell did you tell that photographer?" It was an arrangement that sometimes provoked a good deal of tension. But the Hoffmans perfected the communications system required by their life-style and pulled together with what Debby refers to as an "us against them" attitude: "Them is *everybody*—our customers, suppliers, printers, everybody!" As for "them," they are now used to working with two for the price of one.

On the whole, the sharing of work and child care has been good for the business, for the marriage, and for Steve and Debby as individuals.

"We're rarely in conflict between our work and ourselves," says Debby. "When you're at the shop, you're *really* working. There's always more work than you can handle and you're always rushing to get it done. We're very efficient, partly because we know that our time at the shop is limited. It can be very hectic, so when you have an afternoon off, you really need it."

Both Steve and Debby find that caring for Michael, while confining at times, is a relaxation from work. "You don't get that trapped feeling unless you've been with a child for a long stretch of time or know you *have* to be there, that there's no other choice. So when we're with Mike, we're really with him." And being home with Michael, who takes a daily nap, has created an unanticipated bonus: two free hours every other day.

"Before Michael," says Debby, "if I took an afternoon off, I felt like I was playing hookey from school. Without an actual positive reason as strong as work, it's very hard to do. It just goes against everything you're brought up with about what work is. And your own business! Before, I used to think to myself, Are you trying to sabotage it?" Now in her "free time," Debby devours books, and Steve does the reading for a night course in money and capital markets.

"Now, even if we didn't have Michael, or when he gets older," says Steve, "we'd set our schedules so we each had one free afternoon per week."

Working part time to develop his intimacy with Michael is still not without contradictions for Steve. "I have a sense that you have to do something important with your life, that you've got sixty years or so and you have to make a mark on the world. That's totally foreign to Debby. I was supposed to be a doctor and then a sociologist. I wasn't supposed to be a husband or a father. No one ever expected that. I'm trying to get it into my head that you can have a family and just live, that that's enough, that it's an accomplishment to raise a family and make yourself a human being and deal with all the ways you've been screwed up, and make your child a human being."

But having shared the care for two years, Steve can't imagine doing it any other way, for it's through his sharing that he knows his son and himself in ways that would otherwise be impossible.

> It's been very fresh and good for me to be confronted with someone else's needs. This is really the first time in my life I've confronted someone who constantly needed. I was used to being the one who needed, the one who, all while growing up, had things done for him. But Michael's demands are real demands—they're direct and unavoidable. His presence—just having to do for him—has really drawn me out. There's a depth of love you can feel toward a baby which is different from any feelings I've ever felt toward an adult, there's a depth of feeling you just didn't know was there. Now it's hard to imagine not knowing Michael. Most men that don't spend time with their kids compete with them for their wife's attention. I never have that feeling toward Michael. There's none of the "Who is this stranger she keeps jumping up for?"

From Debby's point of view, sharing child care has strengthened the marriage and opened up new aspects of Steve's personality to her in ways that just sharing work never did. "When you work together, you see that someone else is clever or handles a crisis well. You can admire that, but it doesn't hit you the same way as when you see another person dealing with a child. I really respect the way Steve is with Michael; it feels good to see them together. It would be horrible if I didn't see him being so patient and taking him seriously. It not only brings out things that are true about you; it makes new things true."

Michael is not old enough to speak for himself, though he seems well aware that Daddy is as regular a presence—and playmate—as Mommy. Steve and Debby, of course, hope that the balance in their lives and the time they give to Michael will influence him; as Steve says, "I hope that he'll be a lot more open than most men are, more actively able to take care of his own needs, not needing to depend on other people— especially women—to take care of him; that he won't be macho in that phony way that's built on fear of people, especially women; that he won't be sexist." Then, with characteristic humor, he adds, "We basically agree on how to raise him; who the hell knows?"

COLLEGE TEACHING

At Hampshire College, astronomy professors Kurt and Courtney Gordon do it; so do biology professors Al and Ann Woodhull, and housemasters Linda and Graham Gordon. They all hold half-time appointments, an arrangement that allows each individual to maintain a commitment to working and to sharing equally and fully in the care of their young children.

Hampshire is a small (1300 students, 125 faculty) liberal arts college in Amherst, Massachusetts. It began operating in 1970—after a decade of planning—as one of the most innovative of recent ventures in college education. The key planning document recommended that undergraduate education "be thoroughly restructured in terms of ends as well as means" and "that Hampshire College play an active part as a corporate citizen in contributing to the quality of life in the developing community." Hampshire's policies defied many of the sacred traditions of the college establishment. To qualify for admission, students needed not sport lofty—or even any—SAT scores, but to give some evidence of their uniqueness, their ability to contribute to the total life of the community. For faculty, there was no pressure to publish or perish, and no such thing as tenure; every three to five years the quality of teaching would be reviewed. Even so, when Hampshire opened its doors, there were no plans to let faculty members share appointments; it was simply an idea that had not come up.

The way it did come up shows how resistant even the most progressive of institutions—those most concerned with the quality of life—can be to breaking traditional patterns of work, and yet how readily new patterns can be accepted once they are given a chance.

In 1969, when Everett Hafner, Hampshire's dean of natural sciences, was trying to hire an assistant professor of astronomy, he received two equally impressive résumés. Both applicants had Ph.D.'s from the University of Michigan, both had done postgraduate research at the National Astronomy Radio Observatory in Charlottesville, Virginia, and both had published articles—some jointly; and they weren't just academic colleagues, but husband and wife. After Dean Hafner interviewed Kurt and Courtney Gordon, he concluded that they were, indeed, equally qualified; he wanted to hire both. But he had only one position open. The only formula he could think of was to offer the assistant professorship to Kurt and to offer Courtney a position as a research associate (at much lower pay and status).

That is, it was the only formula he could think of until Mrs. Hafner, struck by its inequity, suggested that he offer the position to both of the Gordons jointly, on the simple ground that they were professionally equivalent.

"This neat solution had never occurred to me," says Hafner, "and I'm a guy with a lot of ideas."

The next day, says Hafner, when he proposed the formula to the Hampshire administration, he was almost fired.

They were very negative. The only solution was the traditional one. He would get the job, and she would be given something. They were afraid of what the trustees would say, and they were afraid that it wouldn't work, that it could cause problems. What if one of the two didn't work out? I argued that we were getting two for the price of one. Then, for the sake of argument, I proposed that we make *her* the assistant professor and *him* the research associate. When they said that wasn't acceptable, I saw how irrational the situation was, how bound by tradition. I said, "If you can't place trust in my judgment as an administrator, and if you can't give me good reasons for objecting to my judgment, I just can't work here. If I can't have my way in this, I guess this is my last day of work."

According to Hafner, Franklin Patterson, Hampshire's president, replied, "O.K., Everett, I guess this is the end of the conversation."

The next day, says Hafner, Patterson called him back to say, "What went on yesterday was silly. Last night I went home, put my feet up on the sofa, had a drink, and thought this over—and you're right."

So right that two years later, when Hampshire Professor Lynn Miller traveled to Seattle to interview Ann and Al Woodhull—both Ph.D.'s in physiology—for a biology teaching position in the school of natural sciences, he said to them, "Have you ever considered each working half time?"

According to Al Woodhull, "We said, 'Wow!' We'd thought about it a lot, but never thought of suggesting it to anybody. It seemed too freaky to mention. It seemed people would think you weren't serious if you didn't want to work full time, and the job market was tight."

By the time Linda and Graham Gordon applied as a couple for one full-time housemaster position at the college, the idea of job splitting was no longer foreign. Now the comptroller's office at Hampshire College pays the master of Dakin House with two monthly checks—one for Linda and one for Graham Gordon.

In all its hiring decisions, Hampshire has been concerned with the quality of its staff, not with the child-care arrangements to be worked out in their private lives. But the fact is that the half-time option has made it possible for all the families who are using it to enhance the quality of their lives—to achieve a rare balance between working life and family life, and a balance of child-caring responsibilities.

When astronomy professors Kurt and Courtney Gordon started working at Hampshire, their only child was Geoffrey, then almost a year old. Courtney had worked part time after Geoff's birth, nursing him and doing most of the other child care. At Hampshire, once their teaching schedules fell into place, they divided child care roughly into daily blocks of time: nine to one and one to five. And even though they found themselves caught up in the life of the new college, and each working sixty to seventy hours a week, the structure of their life-style gave Kurt what Courtney refers to as "the benefits of part-time work."

"If we had traditional full-time jobs," says Kurt, "I wouldn't have gotten as involved with Geoff as I did. The experience of a first child was very exciting. It's something that—even if you read very widely in child development—is full of surprises. And the rewards are so direct."

By the time Sarah was born—when Geoffrey was three—the Gordons had learned to balance their child-care schedule semester by semester, and to set limits to their involvement at the college. "The college still gets a good deal," says Courtney. "It's hard for us to keep our responsibilities down to exactly one job's worth. And we don't want to—we like our work. But we've had to learn to set limits, to say to students or faculty members or even the president of the college, 'No, I'm not in Tuesday afternoon.' If you have small children at home, people are more willing to let you get away with it."

For Kurt, being home on Tuesday and other afternoons has meant having time to explore the wonders of Winnie the Pooh—and to know just how difficult it can be to take care of small children. "One semester, when they were both still little, the schedule worked out so that I had one and a half days straight with the kids. Was I ever ready to go to the college!"

But neither Kurt nor Courtney wants to work full time, at least not now. The opportunity has come up, and they've turned it down, as they plan to do until both children are in school full time.

"I wouldn't want to give up being with the children," says Kurt. "It's been hard at times taking care of them; but at most stages, I've found it very interesting. If I had my druthers, there's lots I'd give up before taking care of my children—like committee work at the college and housework."

We would increase to one-and-a-half-time work [Courtney says] in order to do more research; but the balance we have now is very good. I'm refreshed when I'm at home with the children, and I'm refreshed when I'm teaching at the college. And there is a terrific side benefit to sharing. We have so much better communication as a family. When there's full sharing, the problems of day-to-day living can be looked at more realistically. We're not in two worlds. We function very smoothly, and I think our marriage is much stronger for this sharing. If we had been asked the day we were married what we could do, I would have said, "I'll stay home with the kids and then I'll go back to work." Now, as we both look back, we ask ourselves, how could we not have thought of this?

Hampshire College is pleased with the half-time appointments it has allowed to flourish. "Half-time people always work more than half time," says Everett Hafner. "Just as full-time people always work more than full time when they like their work"—and when they like the institution they're working for.

Graham Gordon, half-time housemaster, says, "I understand the uniqueness of our lives, but I don't feel that our experience in sharing is that unique. What's unique is that the system is legitimating what we're doing."

PART-TIME WORK FOR FULL-TIME PARENTS

It is encouraging to realize that there are couples able to control their working lives so that they can balance work and child care, and that such balance is enabling some men to discover new relationships with their children. But most people don't work in a college as do the Gordons or Woodhulls, or for themselves as do the Hoffmans, or as top-level executives as does Eric Barrett. How realistic is it to think that flexibility in job structuring is possible on a large scale, or that other men would desire such flexibility to participate in child rearing?

First of all, it's important to realize that such questions are rarely put to men. According to Dr. Brenda Eddy of Georgetown University's Graduate School of Business, "Men are usually polled not about time but about the conditions under which they must perform: their relationships with management, the size of their units, etcetera. It's roughly accurate to say that, in jobs where women predominate, they are selling *time*—somebody has to be there to answer the phone or service the next customer—time that can be parceled out without impairing performance. In jobs where men predominate, they are supposed to be selling *performance*." The thought that a man could perform less than full time, or that one wanted to do so in order to have time with young children, rarely comes up.

Men don't come forward, either, to express an interest in reducing working time because they are reluctant to jeopardize their full-time jobs, afraid of indicating that they are not wholly serious or committed to their work. However, when part-time work is sanctioned by the employer, old fears may quickly disappear. When Eric Barrett's supervisor at ESA faced budgetary cuts in his unit, he asked, with Eric's example in mind, if anybody else wanted to cut back to part time, perhaps to have more time for outside interests. Much to his surprise, he found several men—especially those with a working wife—eager to work part time although previously silent about doing so.

Just how many similar voices there might be in the labor force is a matter of speculation. At this point, however, it's even less important to gauge numbers than to recognize the existence of men, not just women, who want to work part time while their children are young—men who often find themselves locked into the breadwinner role at blue-collar jobs. When a course called "Fatherhood"—the first such college course in the country—was offered at the University of Akron, its enrollees included several young fathers working night shifts as police officers, security guards, and factory laborers.

A thirty-two-year-old father of three talked angrily about selling his soul and his time for the last twelve years to the Goodyear Tire Factory. With a high-school education, he couldn't provide a better living for his family by working anywhere else. But now he resented the trade-off between night-shift dollars and getting to see his children only on weekends:

> I'd love to spend more time with my kids, but my job makes it impossible. It may be easy for some college professor, but try telling Goodyear about my family. You think they give a shit? The union won't change things around here either. I'm a

strong believer in the union; voting in the union hall is strictly a democratic process. But I'm one voice; I don't count. When we take a vote, I look around and who do I see? Teenage kids like I was when I started here, and old men. The kids don't have any feeling for family life, and the old-timers are too scared about jeopardizing their pensions to say anything. That's why I'm going to college now, before I start worrying about all the pension money I'll lose. I'm getting a B.A. and a good paying job that lets me be with my family.

Given the current market value of a bachelor's degree, these aspirations may be unrealistic. However, there's no doubt that it is the working masses, not college professors, executives, or other professionals, to whom the structure of work is least responsive. The higher you go, the more flexible you can make your time; as Eric Barrett's example shows, you can bargain with the company if the company knows you're a bargain.

For the masses of men who feel powerless to negotiate, the company itself may encourage new patterns of working time. An increasing number of firms have realized, as they look at flagging productivity, soaring absenteeism, rush-hour traffic congestion, and air pollution, that the lockstep of nine-to-five schedules isn't a very good deal for anyone. Companies are experimenting with three-day and four-day weeks, but the fastest-growing innovation is flex-time, which in 1974 was being used by some 85,000 Americans in forty-five organizations.

On most flex-time schedules, a worker can arrive or depart within a range of flexible hours—for example, arriving from 7 A.M. to 9 A.M. and departing from 3 P.M. to 5 P.M.—but is required to maintain certain "core" hours, such as 9 A.M. to 3 P.M. In some variations, the core time is much shorter or nonexistent; and in others, working time can be treated as a credit or debit, carrying over from one week or month to the next and allowing the worker to vary his or her schedule with family life or other interests.

None of the work-structuring innovations are being implemented with the thought that they will allow men to participate more actively in child rearing. Most frequently, flex-time is advocated as benefiting the employer by increasing productivity, the employee by increasing individual choice, and *women* by allowing them to combine work and family life with less strain. As Jerome Rosow, former Assistant Secretary of Labor and currently president of the Work in America Institute, put it in a volume entitled *The Changing World of Work,* "flexible scheduling would increase productivity while allowing women to adjust their hours to their child-care needs." [3]

Of course, flex-time creates the same options for men to be with their children as it does for women, but these have largely been ignored. However, even though flexible scheduling may free only an hour or two in a day, it has enabled some men to form relationships with their children that are new, significant, and, in many cases, quite touching. Karl Lenz, a fifty-three-year-old administrator at Lufthansa's American headquarters in East Meadow, New York, talks about the consequences of flex-time for his communication with his two sons, aged twelve and sixteen:

> When I was in Germany growing up, the family shared a lot more. There was more time and there was no TV. My wife is also from Europe—from Spain—and she says 'til this day that the afternoon siesta was the most enjoyable part of the day; having an unhurried meal, talking with sister, mother, and father about what happened at work that morning, about the rest of the day. I find that possible in a miniature way at breakfast, mainly because I don't have it in the back of my mind, "Oh, God, I wonder what time it is!"
>
> There's a lot of silly talk at breakfast. You probably don't want to hear this. I mean it's just silly talk. But since you're asking about family life, I'll tell you. At breakfast sometimes I'll play a game with my younger son. Like the other day. He brought home a paper with a ninety-eight, which is very, very good. When my wife is in the kitchen, we make up a script, like in a play. When my wife comes out of the kitchen, he says to me, "Guess what I got?" I say, "Eighty?" He shakes his head no, and I say, "Up?" We keep going up bit by bit, and then I say, "When you say up do you mean UP?" It's really silly, and we laugh at it, but until we went on this flex-time, we couldn't do it.
>
> Being able to sit down in the morning to have breakfast with the family is very important, even if it's small talk. Be-

fore, everybody was rushing around. Now I can find out what my boys are doing at school. I can find out when my sixteen-year-old is having guitar class in school, and then in the evening I can ask, "How did your guitar class go?" At least, I'm on the same wavelength. I'm actually talking about something that is noteworthy.

For every example like this, there may be countervailing ones in which flex-time doesn't alter father-child relationships one iota. Free time won't and can't be used by all men or women to attend to their children; there is shopping, community and church work, bowling, and so forth. In many cases, free time will mean a second job in order to meet family expenses in an inflationary economy. What's important here, however, is not only the possibility for new relationships, but recognition of the fact that men too have a family stake in job restructuring.

While flex-time may allow for more contact between fathers and children, it doesn't allow for equality and intimacy in child rearing as readily as does part-time work for both parents. Flex-time works with or around the existing job structure and the prevalent notion that important or top-level jobs require a full-time commitment. For larger numbers of men and women to maintain working lives and to share in the care of their young children during more than evening or weekend hours, we will need widespread acceptance of part-time work for full-time parents.

Such acceptance is gaining ground in Norway and Sweden, two countries which are notably more progressive than the United States in developing family support policies. Beginning in 1971, the Norwegian Family Council (for which there is no analogue in the United States) began sponsoring an experimental "work-sharing" family plan in which parents of young children work part time—each no less than sixteen hours a week and no more than twenty-eight.

According to Dr. Ola Rokkones, Director of the Family Council, the experiment is trying to come up with a model for the family of the future: "We have to do something about the family now before we completely lose contact with one another and wear ourselves out trying to make ends meet." Adds Dr.

Erik Gronseth, the University of Oslo sociologist responsible for monitoring the experience of the work-sharing families, "It makes no sense whatever to bring the mother into the one-sided occupationally absorbed and stressed work role the father is already into."

To promote its model for the family of the future, the Family Council enlisted the cooperation of Norwegian employers and sixteen families. The experiment worked like this: "During a typical week, the wife would go off to work in the morning while the father stayed home to mind house and children. Around lunchtime, she was back home, and it was father's turn to go out and make the living. When both parents chose to work during the same hour, the children—like most other Scandinavian children—were dropped off at the local state-subsidized day-home, an operation similar to a nursery school which has facilities for children from six months on up."

Was the experiment successful? The Bulkos family, one of the families taking part in the experiment, said the extra time they now have to spend with their five-year-old son, Olva, is more than worth the loss in family income, and they have made arrangements to continue working part time even now that their part in the experiment is over. Johannes Bulkos, a technician and middle-income wage earner, explained, "Before I started working part time, I used to only see my son in pajamas on his way to bed. I was always too tired to spend any time with him."

While the Norwegian experiment has been conducted with only a small number of families, national interest in the part-time working arrangement is catching on; in 1974 all of the major Norwegian political parties have included in their platforms proposals calling for reduced working time for parents—both mothers and fathers—with young children.[4]

Meanwhile, in neighboring Sweden, the Prime Minister's Advisory Council on Equality Between Men and Women—appointed in 1972—has offered, among its major recommendations for Swedish social policy, the implementation of the six-hour working day: "The Council feels that working life and society must be transformed in such a way that every individual can have a full-time job and, at the same time, opportunities of close contact with his or her children, time to associate with friends and relations, and time to engage in studies and public work. The reduction of daily working hours is an important issue to large groups of employees and a key issue in work for the equality of men and women." [5] In 1975, Sweden's major political parties and most labor unions included the six-hour working day in their platforms.

In America, where there is no tradition of social responsibility for support of family life, where individual family units are expected, like individual people, to fend for themselves, what is going on in Norway and Sweden may seem not only remote but highly visionary. Few businesses are willing to create more part-time positions in order to respond to family needs, and most employers feel that less than full-time work is economically infeasible, especially at supervisory levels. Consider, for example, the fate of the Fair Part-time Employment Practices bill, introduced in the New York State Assembly by Constance Cook. The bill, which called for an end to discrimination in rate of pay, fringe benefits, seniority, and so on for those people not wishing to work more than *forty* hours per week, never came up for vote. It died in committee, killed by the lobbying efforts of business and industry, which wanted to retain the right to demand overtime work and to fire people if they refused to work.

American acceptance of part-time work, like the acceptance of flex-time, will rest largely on economic arguments, on proof that it is to the benefit of employers to create part-time options at many rungs of the job ladder and not just at the lowest—where the least performance is expected, where the least is paid, and where most part-time jobs are now available. Such arguments are being made, such proof given, primarily by women. In 1969, for example, Roxanne Barton Conlin, the mother of two young children, was appointed the first half-day assistant attorney general in the state of Iowa; it was an appointment that took some skillful negotiating:

> An opening existed on the staff in the antitrust area, for which I was qualified, but the Attorney General was fearful that a half-day schedule would be impractical from a professional standpoint, and create adverse reaction among other

staff members. There is also a code provision which provides that an Assistant Attorney General must devote full time to his duties. After facetiously pointing out that said section did not apply to me in any event, because I was a "her," we agreed that the legislature intended to prohibit Assistant Attorney Generals from practicing law privately and did not intend to prohibit the practice of parenthood.

We also agreed that, in view of the nature of the position, truly flexible hours would have to be maintained, and I assured him that I would not walk out of a trial at precisely twelve noon.

We agreed to try out this arrangement for three months. I was to be paid on an annual basis, thereby allowing me to accrue sick leave and vacation pay, and to be eligible for health and life insurance. I was appointed the first half-day Assistant Attorney General in December of 1969. The predicted resentment of other assistants did not materialize, and shortly after my appointment, I was given responsibilities in the Civil Rights area as well as Antitrust and Special Prosecutions. As my duties increased and my children aged, I began working longer hours with additional salary increments. I went from half salary to two-thirds to three-fourths and finally, last August, went to full-time salary, but with continued flexible hours.[6]

Further proof that working hours can be reduced—and efficiency maintained—at top levels of responsibility comes from economist Carol Schwartz Greenwald, now commissioner of banking of the state of Massachusetts. In 1971, shortly after the birth of her daughter, Dr. Greenwald became the first female officer of the Federal Reserve Bank of Boston and the only part-time vice-president in the entire Federal Reserve System, working from nine to five o'clock on Monday and from nine to one o'clock on Tuesday, Wednesday, and Friday. As head of the National Business Conditions section of the bank, she supervised a staff of five which had to meet more daily deadlines than any other unit. How can a supervisor work part time? That was the question her boss had when she first requested the twenty-hour week. Her answer:

> In large part, it has worked because, while I am the official head of the section, I actually share my supervisory work

with the other economist in it. Like team teaching, we have team management, with one member of the team being slightly more equal. I also have bright, well-motivated workers in my section who are happy to take responsibility for their work. I do exactly the same job I used to, but for less pay. I also work harder while at the Bank. The things one gives up by working part time are some of those that make working enjoyable. One rarely takes a coffee break or has time for talking with friends during working hours. And, of course, I take a lot of work home, which I also did when I worked full time. I do not mind doing Bank work in the evening. I just want some free hours with my daughter when she's awake.[7]

The combination of her own successful part-time working experience and her expertise as an economist has made Dr. Greenwald one of the nation's leading proponents of part-time work as sound family policy *and* sound business policy. In many cases, she argues, the costs of accommodating part-time workers (including the costs of benefits which cannot be prorated—like social security, unemployment insurance, and health insurance), will be more than offset by gains.

Offering part-time work thus gives a company a personnel-management lever to use against competitors, especially larger ones, in attracting these high-quality workers. Secondly, the firm that broadens part-time job opportunities will probably experience greater productivity and lower unit costs, due to rapid and dramatic decreases in absenteeism, turnover, recruitment activity, and overtime pay. . . . Productivity will also rise because one can keep up a much faster work pace for four hours a day than one can for eight hours.[8]

It is an argument borne out, so far, by the few experiments in which full-time jobs have been restructured on a part-time basis. In 1967, when the Massachusetts Department of Public Welfare hired fifty caseworkers on an experimental half-time basis, it found that half-timers had one-third the turnover and 89 percent the output of full-time employees.[9] In the same year, a study of women recruited to work part time in the Professional and Executive Corps of the Department of H.E.W. found not only that productivity increased, but that "of the twenty-two women rated, seventeen were considered by their supervisors to have made a special contribution or to have brought a special skill or talent to the work situation." [10]

In another experiment, sponsored by Catalyst, five suburban New York school systems hired two teachers for one elementary class, letting them split the full salary.

> One teacher worked in the morning, and the other in the afternoon. They overlapped for an hour at lunchtime. The evaluation was highly favorable. Each teacher found that she now had a knowledgeable person with whom she could discuss the students' problems. There was no afternoon busywork because the teacher was tired. Working half days let the teacher maintain her enthusiasm. Moreover, a teacher familiar with this class and its work was always available to cover when a substitute was needed.[11]

Similar results in effectiveness have been reported by nine school districts in the San Francisco Bay Area and by a number of employers in the Palo Alto area, all of whom are benefiting from an innovative Job-Sharing Project spearheaded by New Ways to Work, a Palo Alto–based nonprofit organization devoted to increasing alternatives to the forty-hour workweek.[12] New Ways to Work is training individuals to apply as teams for jobs, and it is training businesses in utilization of the job-sharing approach. Through its efforts, two people are now filling single positions as city planners, program developers, administrators, librarians, probation workers, and medical receptionists. The City of Palo Alto, which began offering some government jobs on a shared basis in December 1974, has found that job sharing increased the numbers of the employed, broadened the diversity of employee backgrounds, *and* heightened productivity.[13]

While experiments with part-time work and job sharing have been limited, they point to benefits for families, for employers, and—in an economy which increasingly has too many people and too few jobs—for society as a whole. Less work for more people would mean—as many school systems are now finding—a better distribution of jobs, a way to combat massive unemployment and its related social problems.

True, large segments of industry remain resistant to change. IBM, for example, which employs some 150,000 workers in the United States, has no more than 300 to 400 part-time employees—all working as nurses, security guards, or cafeteria helpers. According to Victor Pesquiera, Corporate Information Officer for IBM, "There is an adequate supply of people in the labor market who want and who need the opportunity to work full time." [14]

However, there are some promising signs of change. In July 1975, the United States Senate passed the Part-Time Career Opportunities Act, introduced by California Senator John Tunney, who argued that his legislation "would make possible more fullfilling working and family lives for thousands of Americans and help end the discrimination, particularly against women with children, imposed by the basic pattern of working hours in our society." [15] If enacted, it would mandate that, after a five-year phase-in period, 10 percent of all federal jobs—up to a government salary rating of GS-16 (approximately $36,000)—be available on a permanent part-time basis, with standard civil service protections and pro-rated fringe benefits. If the Tunney bill—introduced in the House by California Representative Yvonne Braithwaite-Burke —is passed, it will provide the nation's first major experiment in restructuring working time, in upgrading the status of part-time work, and in recognizing the interdependence of work and family life. And it may provide a precedent to be followed on a larger scale by both the public and the private sectors.

While the Tunney-Burke bill is being considered in the House of Representatives, Massachusetts and Maryland have both enacted legislation modeled on it.

According to Lois Pines, a Massachusetts state representative and sponsor of the part-time work legislation, "To make this work, it will take a lot of commitment from the executive in the state. This is going to take time. As for the Tunney bill, I think it will pass. It won't have immediate consequences either, but I think, in the long term, it will. It's going to take years for it to be implemented, but over the years, it's going to become a much more accepted way of life."

Right now, it is hard for most people to imagine as the norm anything but the nine-to-five job, the forty-hour (or thirty-five-hour) workweek. But it is also difficult to remember that, as recently as 1915, the standard working week was sixty hours. Right now it is difficult to imagine part-time work as meeting the needs of fathers as well as mothers of young children.

For example, Ms. Pines says, "I did not think about fathers when I introduced this bill; certainly, it could affect them, but they weren't primary in my mind. Mainly, I had in mind the female who wants to participate in our society without feeling that her kids are suffering because of it."

Indeed, the call for broadening the scope and status of part-time jobs is coming primarily from women; the most immediate impact of more part-time job options will be on young mothers. However, new status for part-time jobs should create a climate in which employers would be less likely to suspect a man's commitment to the job if he chose to work part time so that he could share in the care of his young children. After all, as they troop off to work every morning, how many men harbor feelings like those of Mike LeFevre, the thirty-seven-year-old steelworker who introduces Studs Terkel's *Working:*

> If I had a twenty-hour workweek, I'd get to know my kids better, my wife better. Some kid invited me to go on a college campus. On a Saturday. It was summertime. Hell, if I have a choice of taking my wife and kids to a picnic or going to a college campus, it's gonna be the picnic. But if I worked a twenty-hour week, I could go do both. . . . The whole thing is time. . . . Time, that's the important thing.[16]

4

ULTRAPLANNED PARENTHOOD: SINGLE ADOPTIVE FATHERS

"You married, you had children; otherwise, why the hell get married! . . . Women needed children; otherwise, they went unfulfilled, and as a result became deeply neurotic. . . . In short, you realized that you had brought two children into the world on a string of semi-conscious, half-baked, and probably totally fallacious assumptions."—Joseph Epstein, *Divorced in America: Marriage in an Age of Possibility* [1]

When Roger Gatke, a thirty-five-year-old bachelor and schoolteacher in Queens, New York, was about to adopt an eight-year-old boy named Tommy, he told his mother the good news.

"You haven't thought about it," said his mother, who was quite unprepared to tell her friends that her son had become a father without ever being married.

"Ma," said Gatke, "I've thought about it for eighteen months. It only takes a woman nine months to have a child."

One of Gatke's fifth-grade students could only explain his teacher's parental status by figuring things this way: "He had a wife but he put her on a plane and sent her home."

But Roger Gatke's having children had nothing to do with marriage or divorce. There were no "semi-conscious, half-baked, and probably totally fallacious assumptions." There were no missed pills, no slipups, no accidents. His was a deliberate commitment to take care of a child, a commitment being made by a small but increasing number of men around the country. For instance:

Everett Porter, a thirty-two-year-old black attorney from Shaker Heights, Ohio, planned to adopt from the time he was a child. He would marry, have children of his own, then adopt. Things didn't work out exactly as planned. He married at the age of twenty-six and was divorced a year later. One year after that, in 1971, he adopted a five-month-old boy named Evan.

Raymond Jurasin moved to Mill Valley, California, in 1968 to develop an innovative program for an elementary school and to begin raising a family. Three years later, when he was thirty-five, he adopted a two-year-old boy named David. One year later, in 1972, he adopted an infant girl named Alexandra. By 1975, he had adopted two more sons, eleven-year-old Christopher and nine-year-old Stephen.

Jim Green is thirty-four, a black man who owns a small photo-processing firm in New York City. In 1964, when he was a soldier stationed in Germany, organizing a Christmas party for orphaned children, he decided that someday he was going to provide a real home "for a child like that." Ten years later, he adopted a seven-year-old boy named Wayne Alexander.

David Roberts, chairman of the sociology department at Georgetown University, applied to adopt a child in 1969. He sent his application to five continents. After a two-year search, the forty-year-old professor adopted a seven-year-old boy, a Sioux Indian from South Dakota.

Dennis Ralston, an accountant with the Cinerama corporation, was unable to locate a child in the United States. When he arrived in Korea in 1973, planning to adopt a boy whose picture he had seen through an international relief organization, he found that the boy had a twin brother. So in 1974, at the age of thirty-four, Ralston became the father of two eight-and-a-half-year-old boys.

It has not long been possible for a single person to adopt a child. No laws ever prohibited the practice; attitudes did. Single-parent families, which as long ago as 1960 represented one of every eight in America, have commonly been looked on as abnormal—results of pathology (divorce) or tragedy (parental death), not of choice.[2] So for a child welfare agency to *deliberately* place a child with a single person was to challenge the sanctity of the two-parent family as an American norm.

The agency usually credited with breaking tradition is the Los Angeles County Department of Adoptions, which, in July 1965, announced with caution that it would begin receiving applications from single people.

> We remain firm in our belief [wrote two agency administrators] that children both need and desire two parents and that everything possible should be done to obtain a good two-parent home for every child. . . . But we cannot now provide a good two-parent home for all; and we must realistically face up to the alternatives that some of these children face. . . . Entering into a new concept and practice of studying single applications for adoptive parenthood, we proceeded with caution and, admittedly, with trepidation.[3]

Within six months of the policy change, eight single women had taken children into their homes for preadoptive placement, and single-parent adoption began gaining acceptance all over the country—albeit unevenly—from agencies which, like Los Angeles County, had large numbers of young children for whom adequate two-parent families could not be found. By the end of the decade it seemed indisputable in many instances that life with a single parent promised more than life in an institution or series of foster homes.

Actually, placement with a single-female parent had been quietly pioneered as far back as 1950 by the Boys and Girls Aid Society of Oregon, the same private agency that led the adoption field in interracial placements. And in July 1965, the very month in which the Los Angeles County Department

101

of Adoptions was announcing its readiness to entertain applications from single people, Boys and Girls Aid was placing an eighteen-month-old child named Eric with a thirty-eight-year-old musician and piano teacher—Tony Piazza. It was the beginning of the first adoption in the country by a single man.

"We were trying to keep it as quiet as possible because it hadn't been accepted by the state agencies," says Piazza. "You have a trial period of placement to see how you adjust to the child and how the child adjusts to you; they wanted to give me every chance to see if it would work."

In January 1966, when the Associated Press picked up the story that Tony Piazza's adoption of Eric had been successfully finalized, letters began arriving from around the country and around the world—from Germany, Denmark, Tanzania, New Zealand. Most were notes of congratulations, but some were inquiries from other single men who wanted to adopt children. A United States Air Force captain stationed in Japan wrote:

> I saw the enclosed photo in the Pacific Stars and Stripes this evening and decided to write you immediately.
>
> For some time I have given serious thought of attempting to adopt a child. In the past it's been impossible but now I understand some states permit it. I thought you might be able to help me by giving me some information. It would be greatly appreciated.
>
> I'm now stationed in Japan and have done much work with an orphanage here. My grandest wish would be to "bring home" one of the children to rear as my own. It is impossible as I've investigated thoroughly. Single people, especially men, cannot do it. So, I saw the photo and decided to write you.
>
> I sincerely hope you may be able to help me. I wish you the best of success as a "pioneer" and perhaps more will be able to follow your example.

Just how powerful a precedent Piazza's adoption set becomes clear from the stories told by other single men who have adopted. A California man reads about the Piazza adoption in *Life* magazine; the next day he calls his local adoption agency. Everett Porter, the attorney from Shaker Heights, reads about

Piazza and the California man on New Year's Day, 1971—a Sunday. On Monday he calls a local adoption agency and asks if single men can apply to adopt. "It's never been done before," says the social worker, "but I don't see any reason why you can't." David Roberts, the Georgetown professor, brings clippings about Piazza and others to his adoption agency—proof that others have done it! And so it goes.

Statistics on single adoptive fathers, like those on home-maker-fathers or men with custody of their children, are hard to come by. The Los Angeles County Department of Adoptions, one of the few public or private agencies in the country to tabulate single-parent adoptions—and to break those down by parental sex—reports that from 1965 to March 1975 it placed some 19,134 children, 265 of them with single parents, 14 of whom were men.[4] So, at best, single adoptive fathers still represent a minuscule fraction of all who adopt. But the example set by Tony Piazza, carried by newspapers, magazines, and television, has resulted in adoptions by single men in states as far apart as Vermont, Kentucky, Alaska, Texas, New York, Arizona, Michigan, Montana, Ohio, California, and Washington, D.C.

Not all of these men, however, had an easy time adopting. Despite Piazza's success, single-parent adoption translated readily as single-*female* adoption; it seemed inconceivable to many people that single men would or should want to become fathers without becoming husbands.

A *Good Housekeeping* poll reported in 1969, "The idea of an unattached man adopting a child is so far removed from the ordinary person's experience that it is surprising that any significant percentage of panelists go along with the thought at all." Although the magazine found that "62.7% [of its readers] would agree to adoption by a widower, 41.5% by a never-married bachelor and 32.2% by a divorced man," its article— "Should a Single Person Adopt a Child?"—had a special section headlined "Against Adoption by Men," which read in part:

Panelists offered a wide range of reasons why they took a dim view of adoption by widowers, bachelors and divorced men.

Quite a number spoke of a mother's instinct which, alas, a man would never have. Several cited the pressure of a man's work and career, which would leave too little time for the child. Others thought that a man would be too impatient and lack empathy for the child. A woman with seven children asserted that any man who could afford to adopt a child would spoil it hopelessly, for men try to make children happy with material things.[5]

Responsible professionals reflected their bias against men in more subtle ways. Reviewing changing trends in adoption for her colleagues of the Child Welfare League of America—and anticipating opposition to the practice of single-parent adoption—Dr. Bernice Madison said, in 1966,

> In our own country, there are many fine one-parent families; and in the Soviet Union, where the loss of men in the war excluded marriage for millions of women and simultaneously increased the number of homeless children, many children have been reared by single women unrelated to them. Perhaps such one-parent families could offer new hope for hard-to-place children for whom two-parent families cannot be found.[6]

Even when agencies did offer such children the hope of one-parent families, their policies were subject to a curiously sex-biased misinterpretation. For example, on May 12, 1967, the day after the New York City Department of Welfare announced that it would begin allowing single *people* to adopt children, the *New York Times* ran an article headlined "Test Allows Single Women to Adopt," and reporting, inaccurately, "Single women are being encouraged to adopt children under an experimental program by a division of the Welfare Department, Mayor Lindsay said yesterday."[7]

If it misrepresented New York City policy, the thrust of such reporting would have been accurate three years later in Tennessee, where, in 1970, the state Supervisor of Adoption reported,

> We have done some one-parent placements in Tennessee and have been pleased with the results. . . . We still have many unanswered questions regarding one-parent adoptions, but we believe that having only one adoptive parent is better for the

child and more helpful to his efforts to achieve a sense of identity than growing up in a series of foster homes. . . . We feel more comfortable, however, with the idea of a lone woman adopting a child than a lone man, because we believe the mother figure to be a basic element in the home. There is a need for research in one-parent adoptions involving the single man, but this could only be based on many more such placements than have probably been made anywhere.[8]

No research was needed to continue placing children with single women!

Specific cases of discrimination against single men would be hard to document, in Tennessee or elsewhere. A social worker's opinion about parental fitness does not, like a judge's in a case of contested custody, become available for public examination.[9] However, concern for the importance of the mother figure easily covers for the belief that it is "unnatural" for a man to make child rearing an important part of his life unless he is married.

"The adoption agencies weren't prepared to interview single people, but they were less prepared to interview single men," says one man, now the adoptive father of two children. "If a couple plans to adopt, it's because they can't have children; agencies were used to that. But what motive could a single man have?"

The suspicion of homosexuality "comes up every time we consider placing with a man," says Dorothy Murphy, chief of San Francisco's adoption unit, who was instrumental in implementing that city's first placement with a single man. "It rarely comes up with a woman. Supposedly a man is not married because he chooses to be unmarried, because he's a homosexual. A woman doesn't choose to be unmarried; she just didn't have the opportunity."

Although there is no sound scientific reason to think that a parent's gender preference has anything to do with parenting skills—or necessarily, it is important to note, with a child's sexual identity—typically both social workers and men who want to adopt know that it is an "issue to be explored."

"Basically, they're trying to get at whether you're a homosexual," says Roger Gatke. "But instead of being direct about it, they start asking questions like, 'Do you date women? How often do you date women?' They are so uncomfortable about it that, for the fun of it, you're almost tempted to say 'No, I date men!' "

Sometimes the "tactful exploration" of sexual preference produces an amusing social scene. Witness this one reported by Jim Green, who, when he applied to adopt, was not only co-owner and operator of a photo-processing business, but also a student at Lee Strasberg's Actors' Workshop:

> I had to help the caseworker who did the home study. She didn't know how to approach the homosexual thing. She would say things like, "I notice you've been studying acting. You know what they say about actors. Have any of those things ever happened to you, what they say about actors?" I just tried to pretend I didn't know what she was talking about. When I asked her what they said about actors, she dropped the subject. So I said, very directly, "Are you trying to question me about homosexuality?" Her face turned red and she said yes. I made a very general statement that probably everywhere, someplace or sometime, a male or female has been approached by someone of their own sex. After we got through that, she was uncomfortable about whether I would sleep with a woman while I had a child here!

The suspicion that a man who wants to adopt a child must be gay is common, offering a ready—albeit simplistic and irrational—explanation for a pattern of human relations that differs from the norm. (Homemaker fathers and male pre-school teachers encounter similar stereotypes). But to move beyond simplistic explanations of why some single men seek to adopt is to realize how few people in our society ever examine *if* or *why* they want to have children. Parenthood is simply part of the social script, a script which makes most people feel "abnormal" if they don't have children and which easily explains away a contraceptive failure. Unless one adopts, there are no discussions of motivation or competence required. But the motives of single men who adopt are anything *but* unexamined; having gone through a series of psychological exams or interviews or home studies, they are readily conversant with

106

—and sometimes weary of discussing—their own complex reasons for wanting children.

"It always bothers me when people say, '*Why* are you doing this?'" says Ray Jurasin. "For me it's the most natural thing in the world. It satisfied my strong nurturing need."

As Jurasin and others recount their life stories, it becomes clear that their desire to become fathers was forged long before they adopted. There is a mixture of family biography, work experience, and coincidence that combines—in almost every case—to make taking care of children central to their identities.

"I've always been the father; I've always played that role," says a thirty-five-year-old high-school teacher who has just filed for adoption.

Jurasin, who had been teaching elementary school for sixteen years before first adopting at thirty-five, spent some of his own childhood in an orphanage, where he was in charge of thirty-six younger children. "Ever since I can remember," he says, "I've been taking care of kids."

Even when they are only children from intact families, men who seek to adopt recall early and successful experiences taking care of other children—nephews, cousins, neighbors—sometimes combined with a vivid, if later acquired, sense of children's needs.

"There was an orphanage near where I was stationed in Germany," says Jim Green, "and every year at Christmas we would bring the children to the service club for a party. Their reaction when it came time to go back was heartbreaking. That's when I decided I was going to do something someday for a child like that—provide a real home."

But their sensitivity to the needs of others and their early "fathering" experience seem only part of what is a complex pattern; just as important, for most, is knowing how important it was to them, as children, to feel that somebody cared. Ken Finlayson, now an elementary-school principal and the adoptive father of seven, traces his lifetime involvement with children to a fifth-grade teacher who responded to his own childhood needs:

"Miss Floyd was the greatest influence I had in my life. She singled out kids very much the way I do now, kids who wouldn't make it unless someone singled them out. She felt I had more potential than my other teachers thought. She used to keep me after school for homework. I used to think it was punishment until she explained it was because I'd be going on to college and I had to be prepared. I had never heard anybody say that. I was from a poor family. I couldn't even read until I was in sixth grade. So it's a matter of coming from a poor family and having only one person in the world tell me that I could make it."

A strong personal identification with the needs of children leads most men who eventually adopt, like Finlayson, to a child-oriented career or to volunteer work with children. Tony Piazza earned a master's degree in music therapy and taught piano for over fifteen years before becoming the first single adoptive father in the country. Roger Gatke had been for sixteen years a teacher of children with learning disabilities when he adopted his first child. Bill Jarvis and Ray Jurasin were elementary-school teachers. Ed Engstrom was thirty-nine and for most of his professional life a social worker specializing in child psychotherapy. Before he became an attorney, Everett Porter was a social worker for the Big Brother organization and, for several years, a Big Brother himself. Dennis Ralston, a corporation accountant, was a longtime Boy Scout leader. They are men accustomed to the varieties of children's behavior, often men of great patience and understanding. And so, as Ray Jurasin said, it does seem the most natural thing in the world for them to want children of their own.

Still, the question remains, why adopt as a single person? Why not get married?

"I always wanted to adopt," says Everett Porter. "Ever since I was a child, I thought I'd get married, have kids, and then adopt." Things didn't work out that way for Porter. He was married and, a year later, divorced. Only when he read about single-parent adoption in the Sunday paper did he realize that it might be possible to have a family without a marriage. Porter's discovery is the same that other men come to, if by different routes.

When Jim Green saw the orphanage in Germany in 1964, he was totally unaware that there might be obstacles to a single man adopting; he just assumed that when he was out of the army and established professionally, he would be able to adopt —after all, there were so many children in need. As for marriage, he never deemed it essential: "If it's going to happen, it's going to happen. For some people marriage is important, very important. I certainly don't rule out the possibility. But it doesn't take marriage to make my life complete."

Other adoptive fathers, not so casual as Green about marriage, have tired of singles bars and all the other machinery of spouse hunting in America; some, despite engagements or "long serious involvements," have simply not found the "right woman" to start a family with.

So there comes a point—usually when they are in their mid-thirties and well established in their careers—when these men find that something is missing. The need to participate in the continuous growth of another individual on an intimate daily basis is not fulfilled. The satisfaction they get from working with children—as teachers or therapists or Big Brothers— is not enough. It lacks continuity. The children are, after all, other people's children. They go home at the end of the day. At the end of the year they move on to other classrooms.

> Teaching is fulfilling [says Roger Gatke], but it didn't fulfill for me the question of what purpose does my life have. If you're a teacher and you're sick and you're out for a day, there's a substitute. I guess it becomes a matter of "Who needs me? Of what importance is my existence?" Most of us single adoptive parents need somebody to need us. I don't think everybody wants to face that fact. You have a lot of people who go into adoption as do-gooders. They focus everything on what they can do for a child. They're afraid to admit their own needs to an agency, afraid that an agency won't see that as a benefit. That's the way I was in the beginning. I was trying to figure out what the agency wanted to hear. But when I sat down and confronted it, I realized that I wanted to fill a void in my life. The fact is that agencies can understand it if you're honest about your needs. Every human being who has children has a need for them; that's not to say that everybody is really capable of being a parent.

Becoming an adoptive parent can be an exercise in patience, anxiety, and powerlessness. With all their eagerness and ability to care for children of their own, it is not unusual for single men (as well as for others who try to adopt) to be told by adoption agencies that there are no children available.

"My home study was completed in a month's time," says Jim Green, "but they kept telling me there were no children available. Every week I'd call and it was the same thing. I knew that wasn't true. On the radio I'd hear announcements —'Adopt Mary,' 'Adopt Johnny.' In the subway I'd see signs— 'Give Johnny a Home.' When I called there was never a Johnny or Mary."

With child welfare agencies promulgating the fact that there are some 100,000 adoptable children in the United States, it is indeed hard to believe that agencies could so perfunctorily turn away anybody who wanted to provide a home for a child. But "There are no children available" is rarely a statement of statistical fact. Usually it reflects a congeries of factors totally beyond any prospective father's control: the availability of children legally free for adoption, the availability of other people who want to adopt, and the social worker's judgment about the type of child most "appropriate" for him.

For example, a single man who wants to adopt in Arizona during the week of April 20, 1975, finds that, of the 2,150 children living in some 900 foster homes, only 18 are free for adoption. The number could go up or down next week. Some of the children—at the conclusion of a "deliberate search" for their biological parents—may be legally freed and adoptable; others may remain in foster homes indefinitely because it is judged that the cost of the search would not be worth the outcome; in any event, they would be too "hard to place." But this week, there are only 18 children, and he is the only single-male applicant among some 400 couples and a handful of single women. What are his chances? Arizona has placed children with single men twice before in the last year, so it is not impossible. But there are his own criteria to be considered: he does not want a child older than twelve; he will accept a child with "minimal" handicaps, but not a child with severe impairment. If he were willing and able to adopt a severely handicapped child, his chances of adopting would increase.

And there are the agency's considerations: despite the man's willingness to adopt a child of any race or ethnic background, the social worker may be reluctant to place a child transracially or transculturally; despite the man's willingness to adopt a boy or a girl, the social worker will, most probably, only consider placing a boy with him. (The wisdom of this practice is supposedly obvious, endorsed by even the most progressive agencies: on the one hand, goes the argument, boys need a male role model; on the other, men will feel more comfortable in raising male children, since they can identify with the experience of boyhood. However, this logic is rarely maintained when it comes to single-female adoptions. Women can readily adopt children of either sex.) Implicit in this discrimination is a widespread assumption about differences between males and females, the fear that men, unlike women, are likely to be aggressive sexually, and that to place girls with men is to court danger. But all things considered—not the least of which is the large number of two-parent applicants—there is no assurance that he will get a child, much less when. If he does, it will almost certainly be a school-age boy—black, handicapped, or in some other way "hard to place."

With their prospects for adoption so much out of their own control, there is little that single men—or other adoptive applicants—can do but wait. It is like being pregnant, with an indeterminate period before coming to term. As short as five months, possibly. Three years, perhaps. Maybe never.

"One part of you says you should be calm and sedate and prepare for fatherhood," says Roger Gatke. "The other part of you says it is not really going to happen."

But men trying to adopt cannot really let themselves believe it's not going to happen; nor can they easily remain calm. A high-school teacher who has applied to adopt a school-age child talks about his heightened sensitivity to the presence of children and families around him. "The paper boy comes to the door and I wonder to myself, Could I adopt a kid like that? Will my son want to have a paper route? Will my son look like that? Any child I see prompts me to start thinking about the child I'm going to have. I'm constantly noticing kids and family relationships. In the supermarket, I see a father getting angry at his children and make a mental note: That was stupid; it could have been avoided; I'm not going to be like that. Or I see a father who handles something particularly well with his children. It might be something small, something nobody else notices. But I notice it."

Plans are made just as with the expectation of a new baby. One man buys a bed "to spread the cost out" and starts making a list of toys he might need in the house. Another begins compiling a family scrapbook, something he's never thought of doing before, filled with pictures of parents and grandparents, uncles, cousins. "It's just a way of letting him know who my family is, so he'll feel closer to the situation." Hopes merge with doubts: What if he doesn't like me? What if I don't like him? A white man begins to worry if he will really be able to manage having a black child: "I certainly can't live in this community; it's lily-white." All the anxieties and self-doubts are heightened by the fact that one or more social workers sit in judgment of his prospective parenthood. Will he be accepted? Will his life story, the home he has to show, bear professional scrutiny? Might he "fail the test" for fatherhood?

A man from New York talks about being afraid to call the adoption agency to find out if his home study has cleared. "All the materials were in, but I never had any confirmation that I was accepted. I was afraid to ask. What if I hadn't been? They didn't have to give me a reason." He learns, much to his relief, that he has been approved for four months; he should have been notified, but there was a bureaucratic mix-up.

Even with official approval, though, self-doubts linger. As month after month goes by, as one year turns into another, people who used to ask, "Have you adopted yet?" stop asking or become uneasy. "After a while," says one man whose home study was approved two years ago, "people begin to wonder if there's something wrong with you." "Every time the phone rings," says another, "I wonder if it has something to do with the adoption."

When the phone does ring, when the social worker calls to say "I think we have a child for you," a man enters into a kind of labor. In some instances it can be hard and fast. An agency may discover, for example, that a child is "in crisis" in a foster home, and needs to be transferred immediately, and so after a "pregnancy" of twenty-two months a man may get an emergency phone call asking if he can take a child the very next day, a child he has never seen and knows virtually nothing about. In most cases, however, placement is anything but rapid; a child does not just arrive sight unseen. There is a gradual and systematic process for introducing a man to his prospective child. It is not always love at first sight.

"What I really expected," says Tom Bates, looking back to the day when he first met his son, Billy, "was something out of *Oliver Twist*, some orphanage like that. I'd see Shirley Temple and we'd walk out singing 'On the Good Ship Lollipop.' Instead, the social worker brought Billy into a large room containing a pile of toys. He was very skinny and his head was shaven. He wasn't that attractive. He just stood there and didn't play with the toys. I couldn't get him to talk, relate, touch me, or let me touch him."

Sometimes the social worker takes the child out for the day, to a zoo or park where, unknown to him, the man who may become his father can observe his physical appearance and decide, albeit superficially, if he is interested. A signal of approval to the social worker allows for a "chance" meeting, and the threesome spend the rest of the day together. If all goes well, it is arranged for man and child to get to know each other over a series of outings or visits that can last weeks or months. For a man who has long waited to adopt, it can be a period of incredible tension.

The case of thirty-six-year-old Roger Gatke and his adopted son, Tommy, is fairly typical. In July of 1971, some eighteen months after he had applied to adopt, Roger's social worker called to say she thought she had a child, an eight-year-old boy who had been transferred to a local children's shelter run by the Society for the Prevention of Cruelty to Children because of child abuse in his foster home. It had been his fourth foster home; every time one didn't work out, he was sent back to the shelter. He was described as "hyperactive"; for many years he had been receiving medication—first Ritalin, then Thorazine, now Mellaril.

It was arranged for Roger to see Tommy at the children's shelter on a Friday. His social worker would be there; Tommy's social worker would be there. But to Tommy—a slender, biracial child with delicate features and a blondish Afro—Roger would be just another one of the visitors in the group he was assigned to guide around the shelter. After the tour, Roger invited Tommy to get a Coke at the drugstore across the street.

"All I wanted to know was if I could talk to this kid at all, whether I could communicate with him. I guess I looked for whether there was any warmth; like was he willing to take your hand if you crossed the street. We mostly talked about what he did at the shelter, what he liked, what his favorite foods were. He was a very outgoing kid."

Tommy asked Roger only one question: "Are you looking for a boy to bring to your house?"

Roger told Tommy that he was thinking about it; he told his social worker that he *knew* he wanted to bring Tommy home. "I felt kind of excited because I knew I wanted this kid. But it was frustrating. There was nobody to share my excitement with; the social workers were cool, calm, and collected. I was ready to make a decision. They just said, 'Well now, Mr. Gatke, you just think about it over the weekend.' On Saturday and Sunday I didn't tell anybody about it. I knew by Monday they were likely to tell me that Tommy was being sent to Oshkosh."

Roger called his social worker on Monday to say that, after thinking it over, he hadn't changed his mind. That didn't clinch matters by any means. Roger's social worker had to contact Tommy's social worker to find out what Tommy thought about adoption. Tommy had no idea what it was. Although he had been legally free since the age of two months, no one had ever tried to find him a permanent family. The only way that he could understand adoption was, "It's forever. They don't send you back." He was very happy with the idea.

A series of visits was arranged for Roger and Tommy to get to know each other better. One week after he had first met Tommy, Roger was again allowed to visit the children's shelter, for two hours.

"I was permitted to take him out to lunch. He was more reserved. He asked me what he should call me. I said my name was Roger. Tommy said, 'I guess if you're going to be my father I should call you Daddy.' It wasn't uncomfortable for him, but it was a little uncomfortable for me. I had waited a long time for it, and it was happening so fast. A little of my uneasiness was over how much he wanted out from the shelter and how much he wanted a home—my home."

Roger's visits with Tommy were to go on for a period of six weeks: the two-hour sessions were to increase to four hours, become visits to Roger's house, progress to an overnight stay, then a stay for several weekends. But the very day that Tommy decided to call Roger Daddy all professional logic began to break down; the timetable of the social workers began to conflict with Roger's emotions and with Tommy's. Tommy was told that Roger would visit him the following week; weekends were reserved for visits by parents.

"Well," reasoned Tommy, "if he's going to be my father, why can't he visit on Saturday and Sunday?"

It was not an argument to be contradicted. Saturday night Tommy made Roger promise that he was coming back on Sunday, and on Sunday night, when Roger had to leave, Tommy threw a fit.

"He was crying hysterically, and all I could do was to leave him on the doorstep of the SPCC."

During the next week, Tommy started acting up at the shelter. On a hot July day he simply refused to go to the beach with all the other children; his father, he said, might be coming. As Tommy became more and more unmanageable, the agency decided to speed things up. An overnight visit to Roger's scheduled for some two weeks hence was rescheduled for the very next day, a Wednesday. But when Tommy re-

115

turned to the shelter on Thursday, with a hope but not a promise of a weekend visit to Roger's house, he was a horror. No sooner had Roger returned home after dropping Tommy off than he received a call from the agency—if they could get physical, psychological, and neurological exams rushed through on Tommy that afternoon, could Roger pick him up —for good—on Friday?

"Friday is when I finally panicked," says Roger. "I would have cheerfully packed my bags and moved to California. All of a sudden I thought it was an insane idea. The whole pattern of my life was hitting me in the face, and I was thinking that I couldn't take care of my own life; how could I take care of an eight-year-old? I parked a block from the shelter to get myself together. My social worker was parked across the street eating her lunch. I told her what an insane idea it all was."

She said, "Tommy doesn't have a chance without you; he's been through it all."

An hour later, Roger walked out of the children's shelter with Tommy and all his worldly possessions—two pairs of mismatched socks, a pair of size-sixteen undershorts that he still doesn't fit into, and a large bottle of Mellaril.

When a single man takes his child home, it is a dream come true, a time for celebration. When Ray Jurasin arrived at the San Francisco airport from southern California with two-year-old David, some two hundred children and parents from the Mill Valley school where he taught were on hand to welcome the town's new family.

It is a time for old experiences, like cooking a hamburger, to take on a new excitement—at least for a while. In the case of Roger Gatke and Tommy, Gatke says, "We had hamburgers, french fries, and corn for seven days straight until I swore to God I couldn't look at another hamburger."

New experiences present themselves at a rapid clip, like toilet training a two-year-old or going shopping for an eight-year-old's clothes. "In the beginning," admits Gatke with bemused hindsight, "I was going to be the best damned father in the whole world. But this meant that my child would be the best dressed. I would iron permanent press shirts and polish shoes practically every night."

If extravagances disappear with time, opportunities for closeness remain. Everett Porter comes home from work in the evening to play the piano with his three-year-old son, Evan: duets of such classical pieces as "Twinkle, Twinkle, Little Star," "Ten Little Indians," and "Old MacDonald," or Everett's solo of "The Easter Parade," Evan's favorite piece of living-room marching music. Jim Green leaves his photo-processing shop in Manhattan every weekday at 11:30 A.M. so he can have lunch at home with his eight-year-old son, Wayne. "Parenthood," says David Roberts, who adopted the Sioux Indian boy, "is just the greatest thing in the world."

Still, a family born of an adoptive placement is a tentative creation. Until a child's adoption is actually finalized in a court of law—which may take anywhere from six months to several years—the new family, if the placement was made by an agency, is under the supervision of a social worker. If things don't work out, the child will go on to yet another home or back to an institution. And there is no guarantee that things will work out. Above and beyond the spectrum of problems that all parents encounter, single adoptive fathers are often taking on children who, if they have received any love at all, have received it in a most sporadic way, children who have no reason to trust that anybody will continue to care for them. A three-year-old boy regresses to an infancy he never had and must be cuddled and spoon-fed like a six-month-old until he will use his jaw muscles again. A seven-year-old takes three or four hours to fall asleep; he is terrified that he may wake up one morning and find his new father gone. When his teacher threatens to call home about his misbehavior, eight-year-old Tommy returns from school and packs his suitcase; he is certain that Roger Gatke will be sending him back to the children's shelter that evening.

Fears of abandonment run deep and can only be allayed, if at all, by hour upon hour of patient and loving care. School-age children—those most usually adopted by single men—may do everything in their power to prove what their life histories

117

lead them to suspect—that they are unworthy of anybody's lasting love. The prospect of adoption means little to them; some have heard it promised only a year before by two well-intentioned foster parents who, try as they might, ended up confirming the agency label "hard to place."

"These kids need to be loved so much," says one man, "that they test you repeatedly to see if you'll still love them." The testing period usually begins a few months after a child arrives and lasts for six months or so; it is so common that when it does not occur social workers worry that a child's feelings are being pathologically repressed. However common, it is a difficult period for a father to live through. It is full of self-doubt about one's ability to care for another person. And it can be a lonely experience, in which the only meaningful support comes from other adoptive parents who have been through it.

As one man sums up, "Adoption is a lot of work, time, and effort. And guts—a lot of guts, a lot of fear. There's a lot of prayers that went into that relationship."

After one week with Roger Gatke, eight-year-old Tommy yells out, in the middle of Sunday Mass, "If this is what it's like to be adopted, I'd rather go back to the shelter!" Though it throws Roger into a panic, it is clearly an act of bravado, the first of several dares.

The difficult challenges are the ones that persist, day after day, beckoning for some sign of parental rejection, turning home-sweet-home into a free-fire battle zone and making men struggle with feelings that they have done the wrong thing, taken on a responsibility that is much too difficult. An eleven-year-old boy spends six straight weeks pinching his father's skin until, one day, he is smacked on the side of the head. A twelve-year-old boy regularly gets himself thrown out of school so that his father has to miss work. The patterns are remarkably similar; after a hell-bent period of trying to be rejected, school-age children often become passive, totally dependent, then even out emotionally and begin to feel secure.

And yet, as the date approaches for father and child to appear in court to finalize the adoption—to make the relationship permanent—anxieties increase. A child getting ready to go for the required psychological and physical examinations cannot stop rehearsing the same litany to his father, "What if they find out I'm crazy? Would you still adopt me? What if they find out I'm retarded? Would you still adopt me? What if they find out something is wrong with me? Would you still adopt me?"

Court dates keep changing, getting postponed and rescheduled, so that a child who has never known anything permanent in his life is made more anxious because he doesn't know when things will become "forever." Meanwhile, people who know of the impending finalization cannot stop telling the father how wonderful he must feel.

"It's a classic," says Roger Gatke. "Everybody thinks it must be the high point of your life, but the kids are so obnoxious! Then again, you can't blame them."

Even if it is hard going, most men go on to seek a second child; if they are successful, some go on to seek a third or even a fourth. And so again the question is put from the adoption agencies—why? Only this time it is often rephrased: "You've got such a good thing going here now. Why take a risk?" But even when adopting just one child seemed an impossibility, a dream, to most men a "real" family included, if not a mother, at least two kids.

"I feel a child is too self-centered if there's only one in the family," says Tony Piazza, who, two years after pioneering in single adoptive fatherhood, adopted his second child.

"If I adopt one biracial child, what does he have when I'm gone?" says Roger Gatke. "It's part of my obligation as a parent to provide a life for my child."

"If I had the money, I'd adopt as many children as reasonably possible," says another man. "There are a lot of children waiting for homes."

Adding to their own reasons for family expansion is the request that men hear frequently from their first children: "When are we going to get a brother or sister?" Not, it is important to note, "When are we going to get a mother?" Adopted children worry that mothers, not siblings, will threaten the relationship they have with their fathers. The prospect of adopting another child promises children not only a playmate but, in some way, a closer identification with their fathers. Now, instead of being chosen, they can choose, just as their fathers chose them. And so an eleven-year-old boy notices a newspaper picture of the "adoptable child of the week" and brings it to his father's attention with the plea, "Why can't we adopt him?"

Adoption the second time around is not necessarily any easier than it was the first. One man spends two years telling his nine-year-old boy the story that he gets from the agencies, the same story he got before his first adoption: "There are no children available." Another man finally gives up on adopting through an agency.

But all stories are not like this. When Roger Gatke set out to adopt his second child, he explained defensively to Sister Mary Mercedes of New York's Angel Guardian Home, "I am thirty-seven years old. I have already adopted one child—through New York City's Welfare Department—and I want to adopt another. But I'm not going to devote eighteen months of my life to this if it means having another eighteen months of turmoil. So if you don't think that you want to place a child with a single man, please let me know."

The Sister's reply was reassuring and quite unexpected. "You've done it before. You've proved you can do it. Why should we object?"

Together, Roger and Tommy picked out a twelve-year-old boy from the agency's picture book of adoptable children. Tommy, now nine, wanted an older brother. There was only one problem: the brother Tommy wanted had a different idea of what a family was all about. A family was a mother and a father, and he did not even want to consider a home without a mother. One week later the agency called to say it had another child, a seven-year-old biracial boy who was being relinquished from preadoptive placement by a couple who found him too "difficult." Would Roger consider taking him?

Roger checked with Tommy, who, after all, was set on having an older, not a younger, brother.

"He isn't what I had in mind," Tommy said, "but he needs a home, and one time I needed a home."

The agency asked Roger if he wanted to see a picture of

the boy before making a decision. No, he didn't. Neal would come to spend the weekend; if he wanted to stay, after that there would be plenty of time to find out if he had a family.

For six months, as a daily ritual, Neal literally tore everything apart in his new home; with an equal persistence Roger told him, "You can tear this house up every night and we can have dinner at ten P.M., but you're going to put it all back together again—and nobody's going to call anybody."

Outside the house, Neal had continual tantrums. To see Roger dragging him down the street, physically, was not to envy the love between adoptive father and child. Until one day, in the midst of a tantrum, Neal blurted out, "I'm nobody! Don't you understand that? I'm nobody."

Roger's reply—and the beginning of the end of the challenge—was, "Now you're somebody's nobody."

Two years later, Roger, Tommy, and Neal are looking through a looseleaf notebook filled with pictures of adoptable children. They are trying to find the next, though not the last, member of their family.

To an observer, the growth of love between a man and the children he adopts can be a remarkable process to behold. But to most adoptive fathers, there is nothing remarkable at all.

"Some people have certain personality traits or talents that make them more likely to succeed in a certain area," says one man. "I can really appreciate a woman who says, 'I don't want any kids.' She may want a marriage but not kids. Society shouldn't put her down. On the other side, there are guys who really want kids. Some men just care for kids. That's the way I felt."

Or, as Roger Gatke puts it, "With all the responsibilities, I also have the privilege of being called Dad—and that's more than I ever bargained for."

What is the future of single adoptive fatherhood? How many of the estimated 100,000 children in America who are waiting for permanent homes will find them with single men?

Most adoption agencies still prefer two-parent homes. But, thanks in part to the Roger Gatkes and Tony Piazzas,

121

there is an increasing acceptance and, in some cases, an encouragement of adoption by single men.

"There are some children for whom a single parent is better," says Arlene Nash, director of the Adoption Resource Exchange of North America, "children who are so emotionally deprived they can't bear sharing a parent."

Some of these children go through a series of two-parent foster homes; never feeling fully loved in a two-parent situation, they relentlessly play one parent against the other until the marriage is threatened. Others have been so badly rejected by either a father or a mother that they can begin to integrate their personalities only in a home without the rejecting parent.

Dorothy Murphy, chief of San Francisco's adoption unit, reports that since 1967, when it made its first placement with a single man, it has twice sought out such placements, once for a thirteen-year-old boy whose mother gave him up when she had a baby girl. The boy went through two placements with couples, in each case venting the hostility he felt for his biological mother on his foster mothers. The other case was also a thirteen-year-old boy who, because there were no homes for him, spent nine years in a residential treatment center. Both boys would have grown up in institutions if it had not been possible for them to have single fathers.

Looking back to the first placement she made with a single man—a placement which stirred up some agency and community controversy—Ms. Murphy says, "If this had not gone the way it did, lots of kids would have been harmed. We've placed lots of kids who wouldn't have been placed otherwise. We had to make the break somewhere."

And not just for the children's sake. "Many single men have a need to nurture children," says a social worker from Los Angeles County specializing in single-male adoptions. "They don't marry, don't wish to marry. When I first came to work here, I thought maybe it was a man who couldn't make it with a woman, who wanted to sublimate and find a love object. I think there's a lot more to it than that." A lot more. From 1971 to 1974 this specialist placed children with over a dozen single men; and in 1975 he predicted that his department might soon be making over a hundred single-parent placements per year, at least half of them with men.

Statistically, the number of men who adopt in Los Angeles may be unrepresentative of the nation as a whole. Nevertheless, Arlene Nash, who has a broad overview of the adoption scene, predicts that the numbers of single adoptive fathers will increase in the future:

> For one thing, we're going to find more and more older children who need adopting, so we're going to need every available family. The viability of single-parent adoptive families in our society—all the success stories—are going to help it increase. And all of the social and psychological trends are going to affect the adoption process for single men. We always used to assume that in cases of divorce the children had to stay with the mother because the mother was the nurturing person. If they couldn't have both parents they needed mothers more desperately than fathers; and in our male-chauvinist society it was demeaning and emasculating for men to care for children. Now all that's changing.

5

THE OTHER WAY ROUND:
HOUSEHUSBANDS

At thirty-one, Kathy Johnson is the Midwestern sales representative for a large New York publishing house. When she takes her clients out to dinner, her husband, Bob, often accompanies her. Inevitably, over cocktails, the conversation turns to Bob—"And what do *you* do?"

"After I tell them that I do the kids, they say, 'Well, don't you do anything else?' It's almost impossible to make men understand. If you tell a woman, she understands, but to a man it means you just stay home all day. When I say I'm a lawyer, that seems to put me up a notch. I have to have a separate validity. It wouldn't matter if I was the worst lawyer in the world and the best father."

Our society hardly esteems women (much less men) working at home, caring for their children; the United States Department of Labor's *Dictionary of Occupational Titles*, which ranks 22,000 occupations according to the complexity of the skills they require, places the homemaker—usually assumed to mean a woman—at the lowest possible level, exactly on a par with rest-room attendant, parking-lot attendant, and poultry-offal shoveler.[1] How much more do traditional notions of masculinity suggest that a man, if he is a "man," should work outside the home? Better a lawyer, better even a shoveler of chicken shit than a househusband.

It is not just for his own sake that a man should work outside the home. In *A Modern Introduction to the Family*, a standard text updated in 1968 and used widely in American colleges, Professors Norman Bell and Ezra Vogel assert, "A child whose father performs the mothering functions, both tangibly and emotionally while the mother is preoccupied with her career, can easily gain a distorted image of masculinity and femininity." Bell and Vogel are broad-minded enough to concede, however, that "severe personality problems in one spouse may require the wife to become the wage-earner, or may lead the husband to perform most maternal activities."[2]

Like most commentators on the family, Bell and Vogel rule out the possibility that a man might *choose* to stay home to rear his children. Even feminist critiques, in disdaining the mythical joys of motherhood and elaborating on the frequency with which women at home experience housewife syndrome—characterized by "nervousness, inertia, insomnia, trembling hands, nightmares, perspiring hands, fainting, headaches, dizziness, and heart palpitations"[3]—rarely consider with any seriousness that some men want to be full-time fathers; the "liberated" family usually means the one where both parents opt for work outside the home, rely on some form of day care for their children, and share the housework and child care in the evening. As women gain access to higher educational opportunities, better jobs, and promotions, sociologists turn their attention to an emerging family structure—what Drs. Rhona and Robert Rapoport of the Institute of Family and Environmental Research in London call the "dual-career family"—"in which both husband and wife are highly effective in and committed to their careers and, at the same time, have managed to have intact families which they also value and in which they find satisfactions."[4]

And yet, the same working opportunities for women that are creating the dual-career family are also making possible another type of family structure in which the wife is the bread-winner and the husband the homemaker and primary child rearer. There is no accepted sociological or even colloquial term for this arrangement. One ten-year-old, whose mother is a university professor and whose father stays home looking after his own children and others in the neighborhood, explains to her bewildered friends, "It's just the other way round." The reversal of roles does, after all, retain the nuclear family structure, and men who are staying home are sometimes referred to as househusbands, indicating the simple swap within old roles. However, it is not a matter of tit-for-tat swapping of responsibilities: "You go to the office and I'll do the ironing and mind the kids." Just as the dual-career family organization creates new stresses, new gains, new forms of functioning and relationship, so does "the other way round." It means confronting—through phone calls with relatives, after-dinner talk with old friends, encounters with "other mothers" at the playground, and so on—the extent to which our society pins the male identity on work and finds it questionable for a man to be caring for his own children in his own home. ("Couldn't he find a job?" "What's wrong with him?" "Do you think he'll be able to go back to work?") It often means creating a marriage richer in its area of shared experience and a kinship with other homemakers—women, of course—that is peculiar and incomprehensible to most "working" men. And it means knowing time—the sheer time it takes to be committed to the growth of a young child—in ways that can be strange, frustrating, surprising, and, sometimes, totally transforming.

THE DECISION TO REVERSE ROLES

How does a family happen to be the other way round?

Men who choose to stay home as homemaker-fathers tend to be independent thinkers, willing to buck the norms of our society. But what the Rapoports say of dual-career families could be said of families in which the father "does the kids": "The product is a result of many forces, of which their own individual personalities are only part of the picture, the most important aspect being the combination of circumstances that produced their present pattern of living."[5] They are families in which both parents have access to jobs that can support them at a middle-income standard of living. While they are sympathetic to day care, these parents strongly believe that it is the family's function to raise very young children. Since they respect each other's ability and right to work outside the home, the assignment of child care is flexible. They have no grand plan about who will earn income and who will care for the young; decisions about family functioning are mutual, and made in response to each person's needs and opportunities at the time. Perhaps most important and characteristic, the husband—even if he hasn't decided he wants to do child care more than anything else—places the child-caring function on a par with the income-producing one. Neither husbands nor wives see themselves as locked into any one role; each knows that, if he or she wanted to stay home, the other would go out to work, and vice versa.

Here is Peter Prince, a househusband from New York City, two days after CBS News did a story—on prime-time TV—about the life-style that he and his wife Vicki, an administrative assistant in the psychology department at Columbia University, had established some five months before: "CBS News came up to do this little story on us, and it was all very good. They did a terrific job in when they shot and how they edited it. But at the end of it, Linda Ellerby, this feminist reporter, says to Vicki, 'Would you say this experiment in role reversal has been successful?' She made it sound like we sat down one day and planned some kind of experiment, to prove some kind of a point. That's not how it works at all. Vicki had been working for six years. I had been working. It's choice, that's what it is. It's circumstances and choosing what's right at the time for you or both of you."

Jim Carter

Every weekday at 3 P.M., several junior high-school students in Saint Paul, Minnesota, dash from school, race down their block, and then, panting and out of breath, ask if they can "help out with the kids" at the Carter house. It is a large five-bedroom house, purchased in 1972 for $28,500 (it needed work); big but not fancy, and decorated in Sears Roebuck Mediterranean. The neighborhood could be almost any in middle America. As if to prove the point, Carol Carter is out delivering Tupperware. She is a Tupperware sales manager working from her own home but usually found in a Minneapolis kitchen or Saint Paul living room recruiting new salespersons or coaching the progress of a Tupperware "party."

Jim Carter comes to the door. He is twenty-nine, about 5 feet 8 inches tall, with a slim muscular frame and a neat red mustache; like most days, he is wearing a white T-shirt emblazoned with an American eagle and a U.S. Army insignia, a holdover from the four years he spent in the service after graduating from high school. Since it has rained heavily the day before, Jim invites the teenagers down to the basement. "The children probably won't be going out back this afternoon. It's still too muddy."

The children are Mike Carter, aged three, Rebecca Carter, aged eight months, and seven other neighborhood children ranging in age from two to five years. Jim Carter has been operating a day-care home for the last two years, ever since he resigned his position as a sales manager for the Continental Life Insurance Corporation. The circumstances that brought him to staying home are indeed ordinary, if one considers the number of men with young children who are on the way up in jobs they don't like. What is unusual about Jim Carter is that, when he saw himself falling into that pattern, he decided to get out:

> When I started with Continental, I was the youngest sales manager they'd ever had. I was promoted quickly, and I was the only single sales manager. I was twenty-two at the time. The majority were much older; the next youngest was twenty-nine. I was in it for five years, and I was successful. I was as much a professional as a lawyer or a doctor. I took my profession seriously and I worked hard at it. I was so involved I talked it in my sleep. I thought it was the most tremendous product in the world, and that's the way I spoke about it.
>
> But I could see the job was starting to control me. It required too many hours, and I never had any time for my fam-

ily. I'd come home at night and all I could see was my boy in bed. And that wasn't enjoyable. I like to see him grow, and I could never do that. I was always the one coming in the door late at night. Once in a while he'd be up and it was great, but it was so seldom and scarce because it was late—nine or ten. And my wife—on the weekends I'd see her going in and out of the kitchen door while I was studying for my CLU degree [College of Life Underwriters]. I was operating three areas, studying for the exam, and managing seven men. On the weekends, Carol would drive me around the areas with Mike sleeping in the back of the car; we'd have coffee, and that was our only time to talk.

I felt I was too young to be spending the rest of my life in a set job where I could never make a break. And the longer you stay, the more secure you become; then you can't make a break. You think to yourself, I'll be giving up too much security; I'll be giving up my retirement. So one day, I just went and told them, "I just don't want to do it anymore. I'm afraid if I stay I'll just be taking advantage of your time, because I'm not really working. I'd like to check around and see what else there is. If I can do this, there are lots of things I can do. I'll find something that I can fill in with until I find out what I want to do."

To give up a $12,000 job plus benefits is one thing. To take on full-time fatherhood and operation of a home-based day-care program, charging five dollars per day per child, is another. Circumstances had a lot to do with the change. Carol Carter had been taking care of three neighborhood children while staying home with her son, Mike, but she was eager to go back to work and suggested that Jim take over the day care.

"She knew I had a good relationship with the kids, and I'd said that someday I might like to start a nursery school. So there was the opportunity. I knew I'd have to increase the number of children I took in, because we had just moved into the house and we needed the income to support us. It was slow at first, but now I have to turn people away."

Carol worked as a receptionist for five months, then quit to go into Tupperware. In two weeks she had recruited enough salespersons so that she was promoted from salesperson to sales manager. She has been very successful, and although she works during the day and three nights a week, her job allows her to be around her home.

"What we were always trying to do," says Jim, "was figure out a way that we could be together, spend more time together, and where we could raise our own children as much as is feasibly possible within our range and education and so on. Instead of her going to one job for eight hours and me going to another and not coming together except for a couple of hours in the evening, we wanted something where we could live and make money—because we have our own desires materialwise and everything else—and spend the majority of doing it together, at least more than most jobs allow you to do."

Jim is not tempted to go back to work for Continental Life, even though he could. "When I quit, they offered me the very best area that they had in the office. They said, 'It's a waste of talent for you to walk away from this; you've acquired skills; you're knowledgeable about your product. All you've got to do is get the old fire going again.' Even after I quit, they called and made me another offer. I've been back to visit and they say, 'Anytime you're ready to come back,' but I say I don't think I ever will. I know now that I am as good with children as I thought I was, and I'm going to stay in that field one way or another, either with this day care or by starting a nursery school."

Philip Kramer

On Wednesday morning, two days after Sarah Kramer's third birthday, the living room in the large one-bedroom apartment in the Bronx, New York, is still hung with a Happy Birthday banner and crepe-paper streamers. The pigs, goats, and horses from a Fisher Price farmhouse set are grazing on the dark brown carpet, surrounded by "Number-ite," "Speak and Peak," a finger-painting set, and more toys. Across the room, a wall lined with bookshelves holds stacks of the *New York Review of Books* and the *Atlantic Monthly* and thick textbooks. On a low coffee table are some of Sarah's books—*The Sheep Book, Richard Scarry's Best Word Book Ever, Grownups Cry Too.*

On Wednesdays, when Sarah is done watching "Sesame

Street," Philip Kramer usually buys fish for dinner. Since the local aquarium store is near the fish market, Philip and Sarah usually stop in to look at the brightly colored fish swimming in their green-blue tanks. They are a familiar couple to most shopkeepers in the neighborhood, known by sight if not by name—Philip, a tall, barrel-chested man whose thick dark beard and balding head make him look older than thirty-three; Sarah, a small golden-haired girl who whisks along in a stroller or prances next to her father's very deliberate stride. Today they have to stop at the bank to deposit the birthday money that Sarah has received from her grandparents, aunts, and uncles. The local branch of the Chase Manhattan has a large open hall with ropes along the sides to guide the customers efficiently into a waiting line.

"Most mothers make their kids stand in line," says Philip. "I let her run. She doesn't really bother anybody." Sarah wanders off to explore the surfaces of the smooth white stones that serve as a decorative base for the bank's two potted plants.

A teenage girl sitting on a nearby bench watches Sarah for a while, then says, "Where's your mother?"

Gail Kramer is in Room 208 at P.S. 83 in the Bronx, a good half hour's subway ride away, teaching English to eleventh graders. It was what she did for six years before Sarah was born, and is what she has done for the last two years since Philip resigned his position as a Legal Aid attorney to stay home with Sarah, then a year old.

"We just did it, we just agreed," offers Gail, indicating how natural it seemed to reverse roles. "I love little kids, but I realized after a year that I'm not the Earth Mother type. I really missed teaching. Philip, at that time, wanted to get some perspective on his job. We're pretty open about our lives. We never planned to do it for more than a year; we try to take things year by year. I don't see how you can plan much further than that."

The Kramers were, however, on what they call a "ten-year plan." Translate: Philip didn't want to have children until after ten years of marriage. In fact, during the first year of Sarah's life, Philip didn't participate at all in the child care. He was literally a father who wouldn't change a diaper.

"When Sarah was four months old, I started to take an African dance class on Monday nights," says Gail, "and Philip was pretty anxious."

With a law degree from Cornell and, ostensibly, not the least inclination to change a diaper, why did Philip Kramer take on full-time fatherhood?

"I did it because it was the right thing to do," says Philip. "I have a very strong sense of justice, and I realized how totally unjust I'd been. Gail wanted to work. Why shouldn't she?" The income difference between Gail's salary as a public-school teacher and Philip's as a Legal Aid attorney—a few thousand dollars—did not alter the situation. "I've never been the sort of person who believed in work. You work if you need money. We won't be rich, but we can live on Gail's salary. Anyway, people have the wrong concept of a lawyer. They think it means someone in an office with clients, making money hand over fist; not someone who is trying to help poor people and who is drawing a salary."

The decision that one parent would stay home with Sarah was never really discussed; it was just assumed. "This isn't the upper west side of Manhattan," says Philip. "Most people around here are very traditional. They yell a lot when there's no need to. They're always treating the kids as if they have less intelligence than they do. We like a strong-willed, self-assertive, self-directing kid. Somebody else might see that as demanding. What was I going to say to someone—let her be free? What does that mean to another person?"

Philip is now in his third year as a full-time father. Because he enjoyed the first year so much, he decided to try another, and then another. When Sarah is four, she will begin attending a day-care center, and Philip Kramer will begin training in early childhood education at Columbia University's Teachers College.

Bob Johnson

Bob and Kathy Johnson had no qualms about leaving newborn Ricky with a baby-sitter. They were both heavily involved in their careers. Graduating at twenty-nine from the University of Chicago, Bob won a Reginald Heber Smith

Fellowship, or, as it's known to lawyers, "a Reggie," to practice poverty law; it was a trial period, two years to decide if he wanted to specialize in that area or move on to another one. Kathy supported Bob through law school, working her way up from manager of a university bookstore to Midwestern sales representative for a prominent New York publisher. Her territory was wide and profitable, and she was often called on to train sales personnel in other parts of the country. After Ricky's birth, Kathy took a six-week leave of absence, then returned to work. The Johnsons had little trouble affording a good baby-sitter.

For ten months, Bob and Kathy rushed home after work to descriptions of all the exciting things that Ricky had done during the day. Finally, they decided that one of them should stay home. But which one? Kathy was keen on her work and the possibility of advancing; she was making a name for herself, and good sales reps sometimes were promoted to the New York office. Bob's fellowship was just about to end, having convinced him that he didn't want to be a poverty lawyer. Nor did other specialties look as attractive as they had in law school.

"There's no privacy if you're a lawyer. Time isn't your own. That's why there's such a high rate of divorce and alcoholism among lawyers. A big case comes in and you've got to take care of it. It's the same with a community lawyer. You get called at one A.M. because some guy got put in jail for hitting a policeman with a pool cue. To him, it's life or death. You have to go down and help because no one else will. I know guys who love that. They'll be sitting in conversation after dinner and will get a call; they're saying 'I'm sorry' as they're on their way out the door. To them, it's their meat and potatoes."

Bob was not only disenchanted with the life-style of his colleagues; more important, he wanted to spend more time with his son, to share in his early development. He's not sure why his feelings about this were so strong, but as he speaks about his relationship with his own father, his sensitivity to the importance of early parenting becomes clear.

"My relationship with my parents was never good. I never

saw my father until I was eighteen months old, and then I made him miserable. He was convinced I didn't want to be around him. He knows I love him, but he never would have thought to do anything with me. My mother would say, 'Take him to the office; let him play with a piece of paper in the typewriter'; and that he'd do. But he'd never take me somewhere where I wanted to go, he'd never even try to find out where I wanted to go or what I wanted to do."

Two years later, Bob is home caring for three-year-old Ricky *and* one-year-old Derek. Kathy is continuing successfully, with two pay raises in the last year. The Johnsons are planning to have another child, and Bob is not planning to return to work as an attorney. As he says of his new occupation, "In many ways, this role fits my interests in life more than any other."

LEAVING THE MALE WORLD

Whatever his background, personality, or previous occupation, the homemaker-father usually encounters doubt, skepticism, and some rejection from all but close friends. While the privacy of individual family life is well respected—"It's their life, let them do with it what they want"—a nontraditional family structure presents by its very existence a questioning of the norm, and provokes strong feelings. To dissociate oneself from the working place, to define the working place as the home, is to divest oneself of an identity as a male, of all the symbols that identify a man as making it in America. To the world that can understand only those external and superficial symbols, there is nothing to take their place. Once a man takes on a "female" role, it is assumed that he becomes "feminine" or that he was "feminine" all along.

"People wonder if being home with the kids has made me gay," says Bob Johnson. "They're very curious about the personal aspects of it—'Doesn't it bother you to be doing the things that women do?' Maybe people think that anybody who can stay home and take care of kids and not be freaked out by it must be 'different'—and different means not being a man,

134

and therefore not sexually the same. And yet my feelings about being a man have never been stronger."

If their motives or sexual preferences are not questioned, their abilities are. It is supposed not only that the home is female territory, but that the male personality is cast in iron, presumably nonfunctional when it comes to making a sandwich or a pot roast, vacuuming a floor, or taking care of a child. This myth has been perpetrated as much by women who want to retain their territory as by men who want no part of household drudgery. To the sister-in-law of one homemaker-father, cooking is a very competitive thing; she gets upset when she has to call him—a man—for a recipe. If a man is able to take on homemaking and child care—so goes the logic—he may never be able to go back to "work"; once the iron bends, it cannot bend back. One of Philip Kramer's neighbors, a fortyish mother of two who thinks Philip is "just terrific with the kids," often worries that he is getting into the role too much.

"Sometimes I say to him, just joking, 'When are you going back to work?' He doesn't answer and he knows I'm only teasing, but sometimes I do wonder if he'll be able. And," she adds, "sometimes I wonder if little Sarah will really be able to be a mother when she grows up."

Even genuine enthusiasm for the homemaker-father stops far short of any type of sympathetic identification with the role. Kathy Johnson's female colleagues "just can't believe it when I tell them that Bob cooks dinner every night. It's hard to describe their feelings. The only thing comparable is when you go home to your mother's house and everything is done for you. That's what they identify with—having someone wait on them, indulge them. Of course, they really wouldn't want it that way with their husbands. They love to talk about it, but they really wouldn't want to change roles. It would threaten their own roles too much."

The threats to men are equally strong, if for different reasons. A nineteen-year-old neighbor of the Kramers is all envy at what he presumes to be Philip's daily routine. "I think he has it made. Going to the bowling alley and hanging out with the women is better than riding on the side of a meat truck all day, which is what I do." But to actually marry and stay home while his wife worked? "I know I'll want my wife to be home so I'll know where she is. I don't want her out flirting."

The confident homemaker-father may not take the feelings of neighbors very seriously; however, the doubts and objections communicated by parents are often inescapably affecting, sometimes deeply felt.

"With the others," as Kathy Johnson says, "you don't mind, but when it's your parents, when it's someone really close like that, you care about their feelings."

It is because they so often live through their children that parents are threatened if a son or son-in-law assumes the homemaker-father role; it means to them, "We failed," that their sons are unhappy ("He says he's happy, but he couldn't be, could he?"); that their daughters have, unfortunately, married weak men.

While some parents are, in fact, fully supportive of the life-styles adopted by their children, others can't help but be judgmental, often in ways that are indirect and amusing. A father writes to ask if his homemaker son has gone back to work yet, in a tone that implies that he has been disabled, that he never really chose the role (or illness) that he's in. A mother says to her daughter over the phone, "You do want to have more than the two children, don't you? Tom *would* go back to work if there were more children at home, wouldn't he? Oh, has he really got that much patience? Well, isn't that wonderful!"

Not infrequently these parents profess support of the women's movement. It makes sense to them; it should be possible for a woman to work. "Look how many opportunities there are; more than when I was a girl," says a fifty-five-year-old grandmother. But for a son or son-in-law *not* to work? It is inconceivable that *he* wanted to stay home with the children or that he felt comfortable enough to try it out. After all, where does it lead? What's the future in it? Questions that are rarely put to daughters.

A double standard applies to the man who cares for his

own children. If he works and participates actively in the child care, he is a hero; if his work *is* to care for the children, he is a deviant. In Milwaukee, for example, during the first few months after delivering her daughter, Nancy, Sue Reynolds became seriously ill, and since it was during the summer, when her husband, Ted, was on vacation from his job as a high-school teacher, he naturally took over the housekeeping.

"My mother and his mother—everybody—saw him as a hero, as a champion coming to the rescue," says Sue. "They couldn't stop praising him. But three years later, when he did it on a full-time basis, they thought he was a failure."

Perhaps the ultimate rejection, albeit more impersonal and bizarre, occurred in California, where the Stanford Research Institute was contracted to evaluate parent participation in the Follow Through Program, a primary-grade extension of Head Start. When the young woman researcher from SRI showed up in a fourth-grade classroom, the teacher referred her to Art Blumberg, a forty-year-old homemaker-father who was one of the most actively participating parents, and who happened to be in the room at the time. Art had been informed of the SRI visit.

"I suppose you want to talk to me," he said in a friendly manner.

"No, I can't," said the researcher. "My instructions say I'm to talk to the mother. I'll have to go back and talk to my supervisor."

Later she called the Blumbergs at home and asked to talk to Mrs. Blumberg, who proceeded to say "I don't know" to every question put to her. "I told her she'd have to ask my husband. I wasn't in the classroom. He was. How could I possibly answer the questions she was asking?"

SRI never did bother to ask Art anything. It simply couldn't deal with the reality of a father so intimately involved in his children's lives.

LEARNING TO BE A HOUSEHUSBAND

Nothing in our culture prepares a man psychologically to be a househusband, for either the possibilities or the limitations of the role. No matter how actively a father has participated in the homemaking and child rearing, the quantitative shift to full-time responsibility is the shift to another dimension, one riddled with contradictions and bringing with it new perspectives on self, spouse, child, and society. It means having all that "free time" at one's disposal and, at the same time, getting to know the schedules—internal and external—of other members of the family in ways never before perceived. It means feeling dependence in new ways—one's own dependence on a wife's income, and the persistence and intimacy of a child's dependence on a parent. It means the freedom to be one's own boss, and the responsibility to make decision after decision that confronts one—daily, hourly—with one's understanding of a child, one's competence as a parent. And it means knowing the potential for conflict between homemaking and parenting that is inherent in the role. According to Ted Reynolds:

> I didn't know how I would be as a primary caregiver. I found myself in situations where I couldn't be inventive enough. . . . I thought of myself as not being plugged into my kid as much as I should. I think back and it seems like a case of imagined inadequacies. I started with the notion that we'd have this activity or that activity, like going to the library, or the duck pond, or Thomas Park. That dissolved pretty quickly. There were things I had to do on top of taking care of Nancy, like shopping. Those items became as valid as any of my child-workshop approaches. I abandoned the lesson-plan mentality. I had to get used to the idea of a disjointed appetite situation—not just for food, but for activity. . . . I resigned myself to spending the mornings mopping up. The most complex thing of my own work that I'd get done would be a letter—that was a major triumph!
>
> I thought back to some of the things I'd said in high-school teaching, about changing roles in the family, about how women had every right to work, how it wouldn't be so bad if a man stayed home. Just these basic concepts would boggle their minds. But when I faced living out what I'd said in the classroom, I realized what an idealized version of it I had in my head. Without having done it before, it's easy to work out a plan. I was resentful about what I thought I could do and

what I really could do. I had lots of energy, but there was this block. I really had to examine my whole liberal role-reversal and libertarian posture. I didn't take into account that women's work as traditionally defined wasn't a gratifying thing . . . that it was drudgery . . . and that the child became part of the drudgery. It wasn't hard, even with my limited experience as a househusband, to understand what the real issue of the women's movement was, to understand the nature of the trap.

I remember once in December '71 when it got very tense between Nancy and me; we even had scenes right up to the door of the child-care center; we'd be at each other's throats. It would build up over the morning, where I'd crave relinquishing her to someone who wasn't her parent. I'd marvel at my irrationality, at the ways I was trying to reason with a three-year-old child. I'd tell Sue what had happened during the day, and she'd say, "Oh, yeah, how about this one?"

The ability of a househusband to perform and integrate the roles of father, homemaker, and spouse and still maintain a separate sense of self varies with many factors: the age and number of his children, the resources available to him, his personality. Men who take on the primary caring role behave according to no more of a set pattern than do women. Some manage the housework with consummate efficiency ("I couldn't believe it," says one wife. "After three weeks he had the whole thing down to a science."); others with a bit less concern for detail ("He tends to clean only in the middle of the rooms."). Still, if there is any common coping problem, it is the master-become-slave syndrome, the condition created by trying to control a situation so much that one is, paradoxically, controlled by it. According to Bob Johnson:

A lot of people, especially men, think you have to figure out something to do with your time. You get so organized that you subjugate your kids. You have these little shadows trailing around you. You box yourself in. I see this all the time with supermothers . . . I did that. I had everything organized, but I wasn't happy. So you start shopping, buying things to make yourself feel better. The kids aren't happy and they keep harassing. They behave badly because they can't get attention anyway. The Transactional Analysis people call it stroking; if they can't get positive strokes, they'll take negative strokes.

If you look at the things that really count, at the things you want to get out of it, then all the others fall into place, and you feel much better. I don't always have to make the beds or make sure the house is spotless. When I talk to other women at the park, they say, "If I don't have the bed made, my husband would have a fit." [6] I say, "Well, if he has a fit, show him the door. Or teach him how to make it himself."

Mostly, you start feeling sorry for yourself. "Why am I staying in all day?" It's your responsibility to change it. If you feel good about yourself, if you feel you can carve out time for yourself and not feel it's bad, you can really enjoy your kids. It's when you're a martyr that you don't have fun with your kids. People who feel they can't get what they need feel they're not going to give their kids what they need.

It's easy to be lazy, to kind of get into sitting around at home. You say it's too much to do this or to do that. Little kids have so much energy, and they can't tell you what you want, so you have to figure it out.

What Bob figured out was to separate the two time frames: when he wants time for himself, he has to make it, planning the night before for a baby-sitter; but when he is with the children, he is really with them. He doesn't try to force his housecleaning or personal timetable on them. He learned, in effect, to be more dependent, to experience time as something that did not belong to him. And by becoming dependent, paradoxically, he found himself better able to feel independent, better able to feel that the time he wanted for himself was really his own.

In planning to go somewhere with two kids, my rule of thumb is to compute whatever time it should take to get there and then add two hours for jive. I'll get Derek all ready and he shits in his diaper or he's gotten into something and he's all wet. Or we get in the car and Rick wants his security blanket, and I remember he wet it last night and I threw it in the dryer. Or I forget the bag with all the kids' stuff in it. So, rather than hassle and rush, I just add that two-hour bumper in there. There just doesn't seem to be a typical day. After the morning meal, anything goes. The kids have to get out, so I plan my day around getting out at least once for them.

I have a lot of things I like to do. I take care of my plants, and that takes an hour every day just to water and feed them. If I don't have time, I have to make it, and that pretty much has to be planned the night before.

It doesn't bother me that time is not my own. I don't have anybody looking over me, telling me I have to do something. It's a sense of rhythm, a flowing kind of thing. That's just how you've got to look at it. It's not always the same rhythm or tempo, but it's all the same song.

It is a rhythm, a song, that Bob carries inescapably in his head. His identity, like the identity of most homemaker-fathers, is inextricably bound with a sense of his children's presence. "A couple of times when Kathy has taken them for a week, I don't know what to do. I wind up missing them a lot. I make all sorts of plans. There are projects I want to do, and the time is there before me. But I just can't get started."

The rhythm of life with his children has transformed what used to be, for Bob, the fast and relentless tempo of a lawyer's life.

"In my old self, if I had something I wanted to do, I had to block out the time. I had to complete one project after another. Now I'm not as rigid. I saw a great bathing-suit pattern I wanted to make for Kathy. I had lots of old Levi's around which were perfect for it. One day I got the pattern. A few days later, I took out the sewing machine and cut the material. A few days later, I began stitching. I couldn't work that way before."

The constancy of the caretaking responsibility for young children necessitates a new timetable, a new way of functioning. It also contradicts the common notion that women are more intuitive about children, that they have a sixth sense, that they "naturally" respond better to them.

"When I went back to work," says Kathy Johnson, "I had a tendency to feel like a witch. I couldn't help thinking I would be more sensitive to Ricky, to his crying or whatever. That was so chauvinistic! Bob knows if they need to rest. He knows if

141

they're hungry. He knows if a cry is sickness, if it's a true hurt or if they're just pretending. He can even tell if the baby, Derek, has an infection. He starts taking his temperature, and it completely surprises me."

Responsiveness to children is a function of perceived responsibility, of identifying oneself as the person entrusted primarily with the child's well-being.

"I guess there's a corner of your mind that just gets used to the children," says Bob Johnson. "You make your brain a receiver of signals. You modulate the volume during the day, but you never turn the set off."

The continuity of intimacy between father and child tends not only to sensitize fathers to their children's needs, but to impress them, repeatedly, with the very nature of human growth and with their own influence in its process. This statement from one father who has been raising his child since birth is, if more articulate than many, no less full of wonder:

> Being around a newborn child is so completely absorbing. Never having been around a baby, it was quite remarkable. We did Lamaze. He came out talking. He wasn't crying, he was gabbing. The gabbing was an indication of the health, the livingness—the amazing suddenness of a life. I'm not sure you ever remember your own childhood. Through him I was seeing the whole experience of babyhood, the beauty of the process. It was so magnificently organic. I was so impressed by the fact that the naturalness of the development was good, and also that the gestation period was such a preparation for what was to follow. The detail of it was a constant surprise; going from being able to raise his head to being able to turn over one way, then the other; getting up on his knees, then crawling. I'm impressed by how he learns things, by the nature of that process for him. You can see there are things he's not ready for and things that he is. It's not surprising that I know him so well. We've been together since he was born. Sometimes I don't feel we're sufficiently differentiated. I hear him using my best lines!

Observing one's influence on a child, the lack of differentiation, can be a source of discomfort as well as wonder. Parents learn about themselves from children no less than children learn to be themselves from their parents. One father, shy and hesitant at initiating conversations in a neighborhood park, especially at interrupting any of the groups of women that formed all the time, was secretly proud that his child could go to the park and be free, open, naturally childlike.

"I was thinking how great it was that he could go to the park and be free and not have this hang-up, until one day he told my wife, 'When I go to the park with Daddy, I'm shy.' There he was, just mimicking me, and I didn't even realize it. I had to go introduce him and myself to everyone in the park. Now I know all the women in the park and I'm not shy in other situations. It really changed my nature. I had no choice, because they act the way you act. Kids are such a mirror. You find yourself looking at every facet of your life because you can see it affecting them."

THE CHILDREN

Just what sort of impact it does have on a child to have a homemaker-father is hard to ascertain. Sociologists and psychologists have worried considerably over the development of appropriate sex-role identity. In 1969, for example, Dr. Patricia Cayo Sexton's *The Feminized Male* sounded a warning: the dominance of the mother in the young boy's life and the predominance of female teachers in the elementary grades was leading to a general "decline of manliness" in society; to succeed in school, boys were becoming passive, becoming sissies, becoming like girls. It was important, therefore, for men to be involved with their young children, and for more men to teach in the lower grades so that boys would develop a strong masculine self-image. Hypothesizing from such conclusions, one would expect children raised primarily by a man to be active, aggressive, and independent; to have all of those traits associated with masculinity in our society. But is a househusband "masculine" according to traditional notions if he is adopting a "feminine" role? Is he likely to behave more like a mother than a father? Might this confuse a child, causing identity problems like those suggested by Professors Bell and Vogel?

143

It is important to realize that the terms "masculinity" and "femininity" refer to nothing innate in men or women. They are artificial constructs that have been used, pervasively and powerfully in our culture, suggesting that men as a group are fundamentally different from women as a group. Such polarization leaves little room for the fact that the differences between two men or between two women—the differences between any two individuals—are likely to be far greater than the differences between any two groups. The fact is that the differences among homemaker-fathers are great, as are their styles of interacting with their children.

Some fathers are very protective of their infants, easing up as the children get older: "I was terribly anxious about Sam when he was very young. He was several months old before I'd take him in the car. I had a fear of the fragility of the child that wasn't reasonable."

Others mind their children in ways that astound their wives: "If Nancy's playing outside and it's cold, she has to notice the cold herself," says Sue Reynolds. "Ted won't be at her to put a sweater on. With me, I'm out there before she even notices that it's getting cold."

Some fathers attend to their children as much as possible: "There are some things that kids can't do for themselves, and the only way you can know about them is to think about them. I see mothers who must think that's inborn. They go to the park, spread out a blanket, and read a book while their kids wander. I don't understand that. My kids like to play with me. They want to show me things. You have to teach yourself to appreciate the same somersault done for the fiftieth time."

Other fathers wouldn't think of watching a somersault three times; they do something that interests them and work the children into it. "A man can care for children and still do what he likes," says one wife.

Children learn to adapt whether they are being cared for by fathers or mothers or both. They figure out soon enough that each of their parents is a different person and that each, regardless of whether male or female, will meet certain needs at certain times.

"I'm much quicker to respond to Sarah than Gail is," says

Philip Kramer. "If something is bothering her, she'll tend to seek me out."

"Nancy knows Ted won't change what he's doing," says Sue Reynolds, "but he'll include her in what he's doing. I'm the target of the whining, the 'I'm hungry,' or 'I have a stomach ache.' She'll come to me when she wants a project done in her room, because she knows that I'll do it." It is a function of perceived availability and accessibility, regardless of sex.

A child's being free from sex-stereotyped expectations within the family doesn't necessarily apply to outside situations, especially those that are new and unfamiliar. The sex stereotyping of the culture-at-large is pervasive and influential; when children are exposed to other children, at play and when they go to school, they can hardly escape it.

For example, Sarah Kramer knows that both of her grandmothers work and that both of her grandfathers are at home, retired. Nevertheless, she insists categorically, "Grandpas go to the office and grandmas stay home." And when Philip announced that he was thinking of going for training as a preschool teacher, Sarah exclaimed, "Daddies can't be teachers, only mommies."

But young children go through stages where they cling to concepts as absolutes, regardless of their experience, although sooner or later, they are likely to reflect their exposure to a wider range of human behavior. And, as shown in a delightful way by one four-year-old boy, some children do learn early on that men too can be their caregivers. Looking at a mare and colt in a meadow, he tugged at his father's sleeve and said, "Look at the daddy horse taking care of his baby."

THE MARRIAGE

Homemaker-fathers haven't chosen their arrangement specifically to provide their children with an antidote to our society's sexism; like their working wives, they are trying to meet family needs while pursuing and discovering their interests and capabilities. And it is the relationship with their wives that counts above all, that provides support in a role for which they find little encouragement elsewhere.

"A whole lot of the ability to enjoy your kids is to know there's someone else involved," says one househusband. "There's no way of appreciating what it's like being with kids unless you've been there. The relationship with your spouse can make the whole thing either intolerable or enjoyable."

Any change, especially a change in job or life-style, brings with it stresses and anxieties that are bound to affect the marriage relationship. It takes time getting used to new territory. "There are no models to follow," says Kathy Johnson, "so you fill in with your own parents. At first I used to come home like some stereotype of a businessman and growl, 'Where's my dinner?'"

"And," says Bob, "I fell into the same stereotyped reactions. We had arguments all the time—'Why weren't you home? Dinner was ready.' We'd argue over silly things. I'd tell Kathy she was squeezing the toothpaste from the wrong end. I'd get furious at her leaving her briefcase in the hallway after I'd cleaned house all day. Can you imagine getting mad over a briefcase? That was one of our constant arguments. After a while, it became obvious that the briefcase was only a symbol of something else."

A symbol of entrusting one's territory to the other. And it works both ways. It is hard for a woman to give her child up to anybody else, even her husband, and even if she has had relatively little experience or practice in caring for an infant.

"I know it doesn't make any sense," says one working wife, "but I couldn't help feeling that I could provide better for a child. I knew in my head that the feeling was the result of years of television and magazine advertisements telling me that I was supposed to be able to take care of a child. Even though I had tried it and didn't like it, I couldn't help feeling that I could do it better than my husband, than any man."

After an initial period of exchanging territory—what one couple bemusedly refer to as their "adjustment period"—the groundwork for sharing has been laid. Trust has been developed. It is possible to begin assessing just how much change, and what types, have taken place. The likelihood is that the relationship between husband and wife has improved. Nena and George O'Neill talk in *Open Marriage* about a simulation game that can be used to improve communication between husband and wife, to help each understand where the other is coming from. The game is simple role reversal—taking the part of the other, inhabiting the other's life space for a while to get a feel for the burdens, responsibilities, inconveniences, surprises, pleasures. The reversal of roles in a nongame situation is, of course, more sustained and serious, and, for that reason, perhaps even more effective.

Changing roles creates not only new areas of shared experience, but new reasons—even urgencies—for communication.

"It becomes like a workshop," says Ted Reynolds, catching the spirit and even the phrasing reflected by many. "You bounce ideas off each other because the other person has had experience in that area; it's practical, and it's a morale boost."

The wives of most househusbands have been in the homemaker-mother role at some point; even if they haven't, they are culturally prepared to identify with the role. As one homemaker-father observes, "My wife is much more involved with the children than the average husband." Women are quick to sympathize with the changes that their husbands are going through, at the problems they may face, at the rewards they experience.

"We're continually trading ideas," says Bob Johnson. "I'll tell her Ricky's been hard to deal with during the day. We don't try to come to any conclusive answers about things, but it helps. All the little things I wouldn't think to tell her about come out just because I'm mentioning the park, like something funny on the slide."

Understanding works both ways; even if a wife's job is in a field far from her husband's, most men know what it is like to compete.

"All of a sudden I could appreciate why Ted came home and wouldn't want to talk about what he did during the day," says Sue Reynolds, who took a job as a day-care administrator. "I just wanted to repress everything. Ted was a great support."

Changing roles is not the prescription for a good marriage. It hardly does away with the stresses and strains of making a living and living together. One homemaker-father feels himself called upon constantly to support his wife in her work as a teacher. "She takes her work so seriously. Every night there's a new problem, and she wants me to sit there and listen to her. I do that a lot, and I think I'm helpful, but a lot of times I just can't take it. After a day with the kids, I have to get out of the house for at least a little bit during the night."

But there are two important factors in the role-reversed marriage that seem to lay the groundwork for a good relationship. The first is choice. When a woman feels that she can work because she wants to and a man feels that he doesn't have to, each person has exercised a personal choice without sacrificing the functioning of the family; each has been able to reject a role based on the cultural stereotypes that the majority of their peers have felt compelled to accept. And if each person feels stronger and happier for having exercised a personal decision as to what is best for him or her, the strength and happiness of the marriage relationship is likely to follow.

Second, trying a form of personal and family functioning that differs so noticeably from the social norm brings with it a sense of solidarity and challenge.

"Role reversal is the phrase used most often, but I don't think that fits," says Bob Johnson. "We're trying to define roles that make us happy. In doing that, it became obvious that a lot of role redefinition is necessary if society is going to solve some of the problems facing it. It's very exciting to do this with someone I love so much. There's no one to look to, no models; we're doing it ourselves. We don't like to think of it as role exchanging, but role changing. It's not just bad that men and women are in different roles; it's the roles themselves that are bad, that need changing."

Role changing for Bob and Kathy seems to mean moving toward individual and mutual fulfillment. It is a topic, they say, that occupied them constantly when Bob started staying home, and that continues to occupy them—to form a continual basis for discussion. It's as if they have a sense of their own becoming; and, although they are not clear where they are going, they have a sense of where they've been, of the extent to which they've been able to break away from stereotypes

148

that had a powerful, if unconscious, hold on their way of doing things.

"You begin to learn as you explore other roles," Kathy says, "that being taught that certain things aren't suitable to you is bullshit. Men are taught they can't be sensitive—that's the single thing that makes it hard to do kids; they can't be sensitive—and women aren't supposed to make decisions. They're supposed to be doing for others. At work, I'm put in situations where I have to make decisions all the time. At home, it's really nice for Bob to have me decide things, for me to say 'Let's go out Friday night, I'll take you somewhere special.' It switches back and forth. It seems we had such a narrow range of experiences. Now the range is wider."

THE MALE HOMEMAKER IN THE FUTURE

In the spring of 1974, the Scannon Corporation, Ltd., Scandinavian manufacturer of cosmetics, ran a two-page color advertisement for one of its men's colognes, Kanon, in most of America's popular men's magazines—*Playboy, Esquire, Penthouse*, and so forth. On one page, the head and shoulders of a rugged-looking Norwegian, an outdoorsman in a heavy cardigan, cuddling a baby; on the opposite page, in boldface: "**Kanon.** Brought to you from the country where men are so sure of themselves, some of them stay home to care for the children."

It was an extraordinary advertisement, far ahead of its time, attempting to appeal to a broadened notion of masculinity: it was all right, even desirable, to be a homemaker-father, if that's what one wanted to do. It was an advertising approach that, when introduced in 1969, met with great skepticism, according to Bent Rasmussen, the forty-two-year-old Dane who is president of Scannon.

"We have been presenting an image that a man is what a man is. He doesn't have to own a Mark IV or go sailing. Everybody disagreed with the concept right from the beginning. Hai karate was very big then, with ads of a man being chopped down by a woman; he needed hai karate to protect himself.

Today, it's Brut; the bottle looks like a phallic symbol and the saying goes, 'If you have any doubt, switch to Brut.' We know a man is not a sex maniac, as people try to make him out. A man by nature wants to protect. What we have expressed is what a man is."

Just what a man is or wants to do *by nature* seems to me very much a matter of speculation. The point is that men as well as women have the potential for much greater role *flexibility* than our society encourages. As sociologist Jessie Bernard puts it, "[Not] all women have an interest in or aptitude for the job of housewife—just as, no doubt, there are many men who do and would prefer it to what they are doing."[7] In fact, in 1974, the same year in which the Kanon ad first appeared, the Bureau of Labor Statistics reported that 211,000 men were not in the paid labor force because they were housekeeping; by October 1975, the figure was up to 219,000.[8]

Will we see more men choosing the househusband role in the future? Any significant change will depend, in part, on a broadened sense of manhood. Those men who have chosen to be househusbands are, indeed, secure enough about themselves —and independent-minded enough—to buck our cultural norms about masculinity. But even if they can overcome the psychological barriers that keep other men from being homemakers, few can overcome the financial barriers unless they have wives who are working—working at a level of salary that can support their mutually agreed-upon life-style.

Thus, a major key to any increased choice of the homemaker role by men is the economic position of women in society. Anything that enhances the economic opportunities and rewards available to women will increase the opportunity for men to choose to stay home with their children. As Wellesley economist Carolyn Shaw Bell has written, "The next revolution can widen the choices for men and for women, and can offer young men realistic alternatives to the uninterrupted work history, the forty-five years' work experience, that now differentiates them from women."[9]

But the economic position of women is changing slowly. To speed up the process, several recommendations have been made. Perhaps the most radical comes from Dr. Bell, who suggests that the system of taxation be used to make home employment more attractive to men:

A tax can be used most effectively to direct productive activity. Thus, if we tax automobiles on the basis of their gasoline consumption, workers will be shifted from making gas-guzzlers to making other more economical cars—or even more bicycles. If we tax the earnings of salesworkers more than the salaries of janitors, then people will shift from selling to cleaning. If, therefore, we tax the earnings of men more heavily than those of women, we will increase the *relative* attractiveness of work at home for men, and the *relative* attractiveness of work outside the home for women. There are two ways of doing this: either by taxing the employer when jobs are more heavily filled by men than when jobs are filled by women, or by taxing the male earner more than the female earner with the same level of income. Each would have different effects on prices and markets, but either would make men consider, more seriously, employment at home as an alternative occupation.[10]

In addition, any social policies that rewarded homemakers monetarily would allow both men and women to choose more flexibly between work at home or work outside the home. Payment for homemaking, for example, has been advocated as a necessary step for ending the oppression of women, who, after all, comprise the majority of homemakers. Such payments would allow for rational decision making about the division of labor within the family; and they would help keep both men and women from being induced to do outside work that was menial because their being paid money for it gave it "worth." Practically, the problem is: How would the value of homemaking be computed, and who would do the paying? Suggestions range from payment directly from the employed spouse to the housespouse (mandated by law), to payment directly from employers to the homemaking spouses of their employees, to direct payment by the government to families for homemaking.[11]

As economists in our country speculate about both the

151

theory and mechanics of some form of homemaker payment, Sweden is already implementing a program which guarantees fathers and mothers the right to stay home—with pay—in order to care for their newborn child. Financed from general taxes and employers' contributions, and operating under the auspices of the Swedish social insurance system, the Parents' Insurance program (which went into effect on January 1, 1974) provides 90 percent pay to the parent staying home during the first seven months after the birth of a child. The parents can split up the seven-month period as they see fit; for example, the mother can stay home during the first three months and the father for the next four; or they can alternate months; or both mother and father can choose to work part time and stay home part time for the full seven months. In Sweden, as in the United States, men generally earn considerably more than women; however, the Parents' Insurance plan is adjusted so that "even if the man in the family has an income twice the size of his wife's, the family doesn't lose more than Skr 1 or Skr 2 [in U.S. currency, about fifty cents] if he stays at home for a period to look after the new baby.[12]

"Underlying this program," notes psychologist Robert Fein, is the idea "that men and women can be effective nurturers and rearers of children and that society has a responsibility to insure individuals' options to participate actively in their home lives."

The closest approximation we have to the Swedish policy of Parents' Insurance is "paternity leave," which allows some schoolteachers to take a leave of absence—without pay—after the birth of a baby. In effect, paternity leave allows men the same option that "maternity leave" has offered to some women. But it has not come without resistance. When Gary Ackerman, a New York City elementary-school teacher, sought a leave of absence in 1971 in order to stay at home caring for his infant daughter, the New York City Board of Education rejected his petition, arguing that such leaves were available only to those who gave birth and then stayed home to care for their children. Only after two years of legal battle brought a ruling by the Federal Equal Employment Opportunity Commission in Mr.

Ackerman's favor did paternity leave become an official policy in the New York City school system. While schools throughout the country may be affected by the New York precedent, some —like those in Berkeley, California, and Seattle, Washington— have already broadened their maternity-leave policies to include both parents.

Even with such policies available, few men have opted to take advantage of them. According to the personnel office of the New York City Board of Education, which grants some 2,000 maternity leaves annually, as of July 1975 only eight men had taken child-care leave since September 1973, when the paternity-leave policy went into effect. In Seattle, only one father has taken paternity leave; and in Berkeley, where the policy applies to all city employees, not just schoolteachers, no men have yet chosen it.[13]

Such underutilization of the paternity-leave option is accounted for by several factors. For one, the availability of the paternity-leave option coincided with a general economic depression that made it financially difficult—and risky—for any working parent to give up a job. According to Frank Arricale, director of the personnel office of the New York City Board of Education, "In this tenuous economic atmosphere and with the poor job market, people—men and women—just are not taking leaves as frequently as before. There has been a drop in requests for all types of leaves." [14]

Second, as a practical matter, if mothers choose to breast-feed their infants—and there has been an increasing trend to breast feeding—paternity leave is not practical; it does not allow, as does the Swedish system of Parents' Insurance, for fathers and mothers to divide their leaves of absence into blocks of time so that, for example, a mother might stay home and nurse a baby for four months, with a father then staying home for three months.

Third, and perhaps most important, there is still the widespread belief that a man does not belong at home taking care of children, plus many men's fear that, if they do stay home, they will be ruining their careers.

Will we see more men choosing to be househusbands?

My guess is that, slowly, as attitudes do change and as the economic position of women improves, more men will feel the freedom to be homemaker-fathers. Some may do so on a long-term basis, but most will probably do so on a transitional basis. Most of those men who are househusbands have taken on the role because they value flexibility, a sense of openness about themselves and their children—a sense of openness which, they realize, may work against them if and when they seek employment outside the home. As one man says, after four years:

> I really like what I'm doing, but never having done this before, I don't know how long it's going to be like this, so I can't know how long I want to do it. I'd always want some sense of change, growth, of new things. So far that's what I've got; every year with the children is different. I probably will want to get a job, probably when the children are in school. Sometimes I worry about what I'll put down on application forms or on my résumé to describe what I've been doing. After all, what could it possibly mean to an employer to hear that I was with my children a lot, doing the things they wanted to do, playing with them, caring for them, letting them be an integral part of my life? Then again, if the employer happens to be a woman, she just might understand.

6

WHO WILL RAISE THE CHILDREN?

Tom Barton, a tall, blond, lanky seventeen-year-old, is a senior at a high school in the suburbs of Chicago. For the last two days, the boys and girls in his social studies class—the next generation of American parents—have met separately to examine their expectations about marriage and family life. Today they are grouping to compare their views. Tom has been selected to deliver the report from the "male caucus." He stands somewhat shyly at the front of the room and begins to speak, slowly and cautiously, glancing from time to time at his notes:

> Remember, this isn't just me. This is from all of us! [Giggle from class.]
>
> Basically, we all believe in marriage. We didn't have any set idea about when we want to get married; probably in our twenties or thirties, or when we can afford it.
>
> Basically, we all want children and, basically, we all want more than one child. The range was from three to five

children, though one person wanted as many as he could afford.

We all want sons—I mean at least one son, preferably the first child—which means, I guess, that we're all male chauvinists! [Groan from girls.]

As for child rearing, that wasn't so easy to figure out, I mean so far as who takes the responsibility. We all know that the role of women is changing, so our wives will probably want to be working. We talked about marriage contracts signed by both people that could divide things evenly, but the more we talked about it, the more complicated it got. The only things we could come up with were pretty far-fetched, like for the husband to work from nine to one and the wife to work from one to five. I mean the world just isn't set up that way. Basically, it would take some kind of revolution.

To find out that one revolution was already in progress, Tom and the other boys hardly had to hear the report from the "female caucus." Many of their own sisters—and mothers—were now looking for jobs or going to college to begin preparing for careers, some talking angrily about wanting to do something for *themselves*. It was little surprise, then, that few of the girls in the class professed as their lifelong ambition "to marry and raise a family." Most wanted careers and would, they hoped, become architects, doctors, lawyers, foresters, and so on. Even if they had, as yet, no clear idea of the work they wanted to do, one thing was clear—working would be integral to their lives, a major source of personal integrity and freedom. They would have children—one, two, maybe even three—but taking care of them would not be their sole responsibility.

To Tom and the other boys in the class, this seemed "fair," a matter of justice. "What right do I have," said a red-haired boy named Peter, "to tell my wife that she has to take care of the children?" And yet, as they looked to the future, it was hard for the boys to imagine in any concrete way how they would differ from their own fathers, men who, they claimed, were loving but distant and uninvolved. They had, after all, few models of a different type of manhood. None of them could imagine staying home for a few years while their children were young. "Wouldn't that be boring?" protested one youth, hardly realizing that it might be just as confining for a woman to be home all day with a baby. Part-time work seemed desirable, but impossible; their own fathers worked *all* the time. The world in which they became parents would, they knew, be different from the world they had grown up in—at least, for women. As for their own lives, the future was coming up, but somehow it didn't look much different from the present.

It is not surprising, this failure of imagination by Tom and his peers. They have been taught all their lives that they would —or should—have little to do with the care of young children. And they are living in a society which, as it increasingly tells women that they have a variety of meaningful roles to integrate in their lives, is still telling men that they have only one important role—breadwinner. What Tom is experiencing—what the whole society is experiencing—is a kind of cultural lag; our images and expectations of women are changing faster than those of men, and with little recognition that the roles of men and women in family life are interdependent. We are asking, "How can women be accommodated to the marketplace?" when we should be asking, "What sorts of changes have to be made—can be made—to extend fuller options to both sexes, to encourage and support women in their work roles and men in their child-caring roles?"

Such a question is being asked in Sweden, which, in the 1960's, began coming to grips with three pressing realities of contemporary and future life: that the roles of men and women are interdependent; that equality of opportunity for women is not possible if they are expected to add work outside the home to full responsibility for child care; *and* that men are as much affected by sex-role stereotypes as women. According to Swedish Prime Minister Olof Palme, it is now generally accepted "that one should not speak of the 'problem of woman's role in society' but of the 'sex-role problem' in order to emphasize that the problem also concerns the traditionally male role."

The greatest disadvantage with the male sex role [said Palme in a speech entitled "Lesson from Sweden: The Emancipation of Man"] is that the man has too small a share in the upbringing of the children. The ability to show affection and to establish contact with children has not been established in the man. . . . In the modern society [boys] grow up practically wholly in a female world. At home they are, as a rule, taken care of by the mother. During the early school years, their teachers consist entirely of female teachers. There is a risk that the boys, by means of T.V., comic strips, and other mass media, create a false and exaggerated picture of what it means to be a man. The men are tough and hard-boiled Wild West heroes, agents, supermen, soldiers. The boys compensate their lack of contact with kind and everyday men by looking upon mass-media men as their ideal. It should be possible to counteract these problems. The men should already from the beginning have just as much contact with their children as the women. And we should have both men and women as child nurses, kindergarten teachers and infant-school teachers. . . . The new role of the man means that he must reduce his contribution in working life—and maybe also in politics—during the period when he has small children. This is what the woman always had to do alone earlier. From a national-economy point of view, we could manage this loss in production if we can instead stimulate the woman to make increased contributions there.[1]

Sweden's balanced approach to the "sex-role problem" hardly means that it has achieved equality of opportunity for women or what Palme called the "new role of the man." But it has created a framework for implementing educational and social policies to foster more flexible expectations of both men and women and, in particular, to encourage the interest of men in caring for children. A nationally adopted program of "sex-role re-education now requires that 'information on the sex roles be given at all stages' of schooling. In the earlier years, this should be done by giving a purposefully discriminating picture of the facts in order to counteract stereotyped ideas about sex roles."[2] In 1974 a program of parental leave was enacted which, for the seven months after the birth of a child, allows mother or father to stay at home caring for the baby—or to split the child care—while receiving 90 percent of the prebirth salary.[3]

And in 1975 the Swedish Family Assistance Commission proposed a change in the parental leave program specifically to affect male participation in infant care: "Parental leave of absence with full insurance benefit is to be prolonged from seven to eight months. This time off from work will be divided so that at least one month of the leave is earmarked for the father. If he doesn't avail himself of his part of the time, the family forfeits a benefit." [4]

In our country—where employers are still reluctant to pay maternity benefits—parental leave or other policies of encouraging male involvement in child rearing have scarcely been broached for serious national consideration. In fact, our only policies which even address the role of men in family life are punitive ones, geared to tracking down "runaway fathers" whose children constitute a national welfare cost. To the extent that our policymakers are concerned with the care of children (and there is, to be sure, not an overwhelming deal of concern), their focus, almost exclusively, is on the "working mother," with no consideration that "working fathers" could earn income *and* participate in the rearing of their children.

It was most unusual, then, at 1973 Senate hearings on "American Families: Trends and Pressures"—hearings called by Senator Walter Mondale to examine those aspects of family life most demanding of public attention—when sociologist Jessie Bernard singled out the potential role of men in child rearing as one of the most crucial—and neglected—issues of public policy:

> In considering the impact of legislation on the family, I would like to emphasize the importance of including the impact of such legislation on fathers. I am not here referring to the situation in which fathers desert, a topic I do not mean to minimize, but one which we are all-too-well aware of and to which many talented people are devoting their attention. I would like rather to call attention to the millions of fathers who, though they do not physically desert their families nevertheless, in effect, renege on their contribution to child rearing. They far outnumber the deserting fathers.

It is all too easy for us to see the mote in the other person's eye and not the beam in our own. I respectfully call attention here to the families of men in this very Congress, in our industries, in our universities and colleges. I call attention, in fact, to most fathers in this country. Their contribution to the rearing of children is minimal.

The trend of the times is in the direction of greater sharing of the child-rearing function by both parents. Interviews with young women of both college and high school age report them as looking forward to marrying men who will be willing to assume their share of the responsibility of parenthood. Young men are also showing a willingness to do so. In one study, as many as a third of the young men studied were "highly positive" to the idea not only of having children but also of rearing them. Anything that involves fathers in child rearing should be encouraged.

The kinds of legislation relevant in this matter would perhaps be largely those dealing with hours of labor and educational curricula. But anything that broke down the restraints imposed by unrealistic role stereotypes could be helpful in making it possible for fathers to participate more in child rearing.[5]

But what sorts of changes are possible? How can the effects of sex stereotyping, so ingrained in our culture, be overcome in a way that encourages men to participate in child care?

The changes most likely to promote male involvement in child rearing are economic ones, ones that would allow men and women to meet their child-care needs flexibly, without compromising on family income: restructuring of working time, parental leaves with guaranteed employment on return, payments for work done in the home, guaranteed income policies, and, perhaps most significantly, anything that would improve the economic opportunity and status of women. The more women work outside the home and gain significant economic independence the more will they say, "Why should we have all the responsibility for child care?" In some families, undoubtedly, this will present a threat. But in others, the economic independence of women will make it possible for men, relieved from the pressures of exclusive breadwinning, to begin discovering relationships with their children that their own fathers never imagined possible.

As important as they are, though, large-scale economic changes are only part of the solution. Long before they become parents, boys (and girls) absorb the cultural message that it is only females who can or should be nurturant care givers. So it is only by changing that message—throughout the whole life cycle—that we will begin to give youth like Tom Barton and his classmates a broader sense of nurturant manhood. There are no quick and easy ways to do this. The measures outlined below are modest, especially when compared to some of the economic and legal changes described elsewhere in this book. But they further suggest the need for balancing our approach to the "sex-role problem." And they point, however modestly, to some ways for counteracting the effects of a culture that prepares men—all their lives—for neither the responsibility nor the opportunity of caring for children.

SEX-ROLE REEDUCATION: THE EARLY YEARS

Even before they can read, children begin learning—and absorbing—sex-role differences. The picture books of the nursery school, and subsequently the reading primers of the kindergarten and the textbooks of the elementary school, are one major way in which we transmit the cultural script about child rearing.

One of the important results of the women's movement has been the appearance over the last few years of books telling children that, yes, mommies do work out of the home as well as care for their young. In Joe Lasker's *Mommies Can Be Anything*, they are attorneys, doctors, and astronauts; and in Eve Merriam's *Mommies at Work*, they are letter carriers, television producers, and police officers. It is a list that is—and should be—expanding.

If children's books are broadening the image of women, the pace of change is not the same for men. Most still convey the impression that child rearing is a very special function—the dailiness of which can only be managed by women. Rarely is there a sense that boys have an interest in taking care of children, or that when they grow to be men, they will share actively in parenthood.

Not that fatherhood isn't represented. As feminist analyses of children's literature have noted, it is but one of a wide range of roles open to men, including balloonist, ski teacher, space station worker, submarine operator, forest ranger, electrician, and expert on art. Still, from most father-child episodes in children's books, one could easily surmise that all men are divorced —none with custody—that they have visiting privileges only on weekends, and that all they know how to do with children is take them to parks, zoos, and ice-cream stands.[6]

Usually when men take on a fuller presence in the lives of their children, the message is that they have become mothers. In Robert Stewart's *The Daddy Book*, published in 1972, fathers of all races and occupations interact warmly with their children; but when it comes to the daily responsibilities involved in child care—changing diapers, cooking dinner, washing dishes, giving baths—"Daddy often does what Mommy does." If they are not imitating mothers, fathers take on routine child care because they are filling in for mothers. In one of Charlotte Zolotow's books, a father takes care of his young daughter all day, bathes her, puts her to bed, and then responds gently to her bedtime restlessness; the name of the book is *The Night When Mother Was Away*.

The fact is that fathers care for their children in a variety of ways, not just because they are imitating or pinch-hitting for mother, but because they want to, because they are parents. Just as children's books have denied that some 40 percent of women work outside the home, so they have denied the fuller roles that men play—or can play—in child rearing.

A few books are, however, starting to depict men in more intimate contact with children. *Martin's Father*, published by the feminist collective Lollipop Power, takes us through the routine that preschooler Martin shares with his dad (there's no mother present). After father cooks breakfast for them, they do the laundry, go for a walk, make sandwiches, and so forth, until bedtime: "And last of all, he played a tune on Martin's

162

xylophone, every evening the same one." As a work of literature, *Martin's Father* is not very engaging; but given the absence of books showing men in caring roles, it is an important beginning.

Zeek Silver Moon by Amy Ehrlich is a superb piece of literature, and one of the rare books to capture the spontaneous flow of feeling between father and child. When baby Zeek is born, his father makes him a cradle and, in a scene unique for children's books, makes up a lullaby for singing him to sleep. There is more to this father-son relationship than roughhousing or Little League; mother and father share equally and naturally in the fun of being with Zeek (his laughter when shaking out a rug in the living room, his curiosity) and in their responsibilities as parents (cooking, washing, disciplining).

The only book (as of this writing) to show a homemaker-father, *Hello, Aurora*, was published in Norway in 1966 and brought to America in English translation eight years later. In the Tege family, father takes care of six-year-old Aurora and six-month old Socrates, while mother practices law in Oslo. Even in Norway, it is an unusual life-style, and the book explores sensitively and humorously, from Aurora's viewpoint, what it feels like to be doing something that is natural, sensible, *and* at odds with the culture's norm about childrearing.

To show children that it is possible and even quite normal for men to be involved in child care, it is not necessary to publish a batch of books about role-reversed marriages. But it is important, if we are going to break down stereotypes about men as well as women, to show children images of the variety of life-styles that men have, varying all the way from the father who never sees his children because he is working all the time and the father who sees his children only on the weekend because he is divorced and without custody, to the single adoptive father, the homemaker-father, the father with custody, and the father who shares in the child rearing. Nor is it just as fathers that we should show men involved with young children. In only a few books do young children have male preschool or day-care teachers (*Joshua's Day*, published by Lollipop Power, is one), and despite several books now showing female doctors, there are no books with male pediatric nurses. To help correct this situation I took a number of photographs, as I traveled around the country, of male nurses and teachers and of fathers interacting with their children. These "Resource Photos of Men in the Nurturing Role" are now available, along with many other materials for developing a nonsexist early childhood curriculum, from the Women's Action Alliance Non-Sexist Early Education Project, 370 Lexington Avenue, New York City, N.Y. 10017.

The books and photos we offer our children are not their only source of ideas about what the world is like; but they are one way in which we can begin showing them what is possible.

CREATING OPPORTUNITIES TO CARE FOR YOUNG CHILDREN

Unless he comes from a large family, a boy growing up in our society may never have occasion to think about the care of young children. His sister may baby-sit the neighbor's kids, but he will mow their lawn. And by the time he's in junior high, he's learned not to be caught playing with little kids lest his friends think him a sissy.

Ed Downey, a senior at a high school in Florida, learned all these rules of boyhood. He did, indeed, mow the lawn while his sister baby-sat; and until this year he planned, upon graduating, to work in his father's restaurant business. But now his plans have changed; he may eventually go to work for the family business, but next year, at least, he will work as an assistant teacher in a local kindergarten.

Why the change? Because last year Ed, like some 15,000 other junior and senior high-school students across the country, took part in an experimental program called "Exploring Childhood." Sponsored by the federal Office of Child Development, it allows students to receive academic credit for "field work" done in preschools, day-care centers, and elementary schools. Last year Ed spent four hours each week in his high-school class learning about theories of child development and about how other societies rear their children; even more significantly, he spent another ten hours a week in a nearby elementary school.

"It was a fantastic experience," he says. "I guess I didn't just learn about kids. I learned about myself. That I was really good at teaching them. You know, this is the only class in high school where I've ever felt successful—where I've really done something."

Randy Marx, a junior at a high school in Pennsylvania, was the only boy to sign up when the Exploring Childhood program was offered through the Home Economics Department: "Me and seventeen girls. Did I ever take shit for that. You know, they called me queer, faggot, things like that. I tried to let it roll off my back. I figured, that's their hang-up, not mine. But it bothered me; I won't say it didn't. Then, after they saw what I was doing, they started getting interested. Six guys I know are signed up for the course next year."

Exploring Childhood was not developed specifically to recruit high-school boys, but to teach adolescents about child development. However, statistics from the Education Development Center, which is contracted to direct the nationwide program, confirm the increased trend of male enrollment. During its first year of operation, EDC mandated 20 percent male enrollment from all participating schools, many of which had to struggle to meet the quota. During the second year, with no quota required, all schools met the 20 percent mark.

Just what effect participation in Exploring Childhood will have on the parenting behavior of Ed or Randy (or any other students, male or female) cannot yet be determined. But the program demonstrates how readily stereotypes can be broken down—once we say it's O.K. for boys to be taking care of little kids.

We need to create more such opportunities—long before the high-school years. We could begin, for example, in the elementary grades by having older children—fourth, fifth, and sixth graders—do field work in the kindergarten class or, preferably, in local preschools and day-care centers. The role that elementary-school children could play in a day-care center would be different, of course, from that of high-school students;

they would need considerable supervision themselves. But in many communities, school-age children elect to be on the traffic patrol helping younger children cross the street to school. When working with younger children becomes a privilege, we will be taking another modest step in affecting the way our society thinks about the importance of child *caring*.

BROADENING THE SCOPE OF CAREER COUNSELING: A NEW LIFE PLAN FOR WOMEN—AND FOR MEN

When Betty Friedan published *The Feminine Mystique* in 1963 and helped rejuvenate the women's movement in America, she called for

> a drastic reshaping of the cultural image of femininity that will permit women to reach maturity, identity, completeness of self, without conflict with sexual fulfillment. A massive attempt must be made by educators, manipulators, guidance counselors—to stop the early marriage movement, stop girls from growing up wanting to be "just a housewife," stop it by insisting, with the same attention from childhood on that parents and educators give to boys, that girls develop the resources of self, goals that will permit them to find their own identity. . . . Educators at every women's college, at every university, junior college, and community college must see to it that women make a lifetime commitment (call it a "life plan," a "vocation," a "life purpose" if that dirty word *career* has too many celibate connotations) to a field of thought, to work of serious importance to society.[7]

While the "drastic reshaping of the cultural image of femininity" is hardly complete, the effort is well under way—significantly so in attempts to eliminate sex bias from career counseling. Consider that, at the time of Ms. Friedan's declaration, the Strong Vocational Interest Blank, one of the tests most widely used in counseling college-ability students, offered guidance counselors the following advice in interpreting test results:

> Many young women do not appear to have strong occupational or career interests, and they may score high only in

166

certain "premarital" occupations: elementary school teacher, office worker, stenographer-secretary. Such a finding is disappointing to many college women, since they are likely to consider themselves career oriented. In such cases, the selection of an area of training or an occupation should probably be based upon practical considerations—fields providing backgrounds that might be helpful to a wife and mother, occupations that can be pursued part-time, are easily resumed after periods of nonemployment, and are readily available in different locales.[8]

Such advice may have been gratuitous. The test itself allowed women to express little interest in other than premarital occupations. Men and women received different test forms, and whatever likes and dislikes they marked on the test were filtered through a sexist screen; women could be told they displayed interest in being stenographer-secretaries but not production managers, laboratory technicians but not pharmacists, office workers but not public administrators.

Pressure for the elimination of sex bias in the Strong and other vocational tests mounted during the late 1960's and reached a head in 1972 at the national convention of the American Personnel and Guidance Association, the major organization for professionals in the counseling field. A Commission on Sex Bias in Measurement was appointed and charged to "petition and negotiate for the elimination of discrimination from the Strong."[9] Meanwhile, the National Institute of Education was appointing a commission on sex bias in measurement. Dr. David Campbell, the test's principle architect, acknowledged that it did "tend to perpetuate stereotyped roles for men and women at the expense of women."[10]

In 1974, barely a decade after *The Feminine Mystique* appeared, a new version of the Strong was published. It didn't go as far as some critics hoped, but it combined previously separate male and female test forms into one form undifferentiated for gender, eliminated all wording that implied job specification by sex (e.g., police officer vs. policeman), and extended and equalized the range of options in which men and women could express an interest.[11]

167

Even while the Strong was being revised, the National Institute of Education and other organizations were sponsoring workshops throughout the country to teach counselors and counselor-trainers how to recognize and deal with sex bias in the tests they administered *and* in themselves. A counselor at Long Island University, which serves a large blue-collar population, says,

> If a girl comes in and says she wants to be a nurse, I ask her why she doesn't want to be a doctor. There may be genuine reasons like lack of finances or interest or even a lack of ability to stick it out that long in school. But there also may be excuses, rationales for taking on a challenge that doesn't seem right for a woman, even though other women are doing it. She may be worried about the conflict with taking care of children she doesn't even have; she might not even be married! I try to help her realize what *she* wants, and then we explore the different ways of getting there.

While there is a long way to go in eliminating sex bias against women from career counseling, in helping them to develop a new "life plan," there is another type of sex bias, so thoroughly ingrained—so much a part of our culture—that efforts to reform testing and counseling hardly broach it. The premise of our society is that men should work, full time if possible, at as high a level of earnings as possible from graduation to retirement without any years out. It has never been assumed that a man's career outlook could or should be affected if he became a father, nor has it been suggested—in all the efforts to eliminate sex bias in career counseling—that we consider a new "life plan" for men, one that recognizes the possibility of child-caring responsibilities or desires. For a counselor to suggest that a male client plan a career with some thought to the balance between work and home life would be, would it not, an application to men of the same type of sex bias from which we are trying to free women? "Yes," says the counselor. "And, besides, it is not my concern how anybody organizes his or her family life."

But apparently it is nobody's concern, at least until marriage counselors help men understand why and how they have managed to strain their marriages and become strangers to their children, or until psychologists—increasingly being hired by large corporations—help men through a mid-life crisis. Our society's concern with the interplay between work and family life is retrospective, usually occurring when there is some form of family breakdown. There is no professional group, in the schools or elsewhere, helping young people, and males in particular, to develop a broader perspective on career planning, one that includes consideration of the roles other than breadwinner that are personally fulfilling and supportive of family life.

Concern for child care should not be a constraint on the career planning of women or men; nor should it by any means suggest that all men and women should have children. The point is that if we are going to encourage men and women in their working and their nurturing roles, we have to begin finding ways—perhaps in our counseling methods, perhaps in our social studies curricula—to help young people develop an awareness (other than that derived in their own families) of how life-styles are shaped. We should invite men and women to share with young people the decision-making processes that have gone into the creation of a variety of family styles— styles that have been functional and nonfunctional. In effect, we should realize that, if we are going to guide people to careers, we should help them become aware that in many cases those careers will be negotiated along with decisions about family life.

FAMILY-CENTERED CHILDBIRTH

"I'm sure I couldn't prove this in any way," says Martin Hammond, "but just being there when Sally was born makes me feel closer to her. I can't imagine not being there. In fact, I can't imagine why men haven't always been present at the birth of their children."

Over the last twenty to twenty-five years, with the publication of such pioneering books as Grantly Dick Read's *Childbirth Without Fear*, Marjorie Karmel's *Thank You, Dr. Lamaze*, and Robert Bradley's *Husband-Coached Childbirth* and with a

169

national movement of childbirth education, childbearing has undergone a radical transformation; more and more women are now giving birth to their children without anesthesia and *with* the active support of their husbands. For women, it has been a chance to gain control of their own bodies; and for men, it has been a chance to share in one of life's most remarkable experiences.

The transformation has hardly been complete. In most hospitals, childbirth is still a private affair between a woman and her usually male obstetrician; expectant fathers pace anxiously up and down hospital corridors, waiting for the doctor to announce the new arrival. The rationale for not allowing fathers into the delivery room is usually that they might be squeamish and faint, that they might interfere with the delivery. In others, fathers are allowed into the delivery room, but then, in the days following birth, not allowed to do any more than see their infants through a nursery window. Here, the rationale seems to be that, since they can't lactate, fathers don't count as much as mothers in the days after birth.

The feelings of deprivation men can experience when excluded from childbirth are often overlooked, but they can run deep. Consider the case of Earl Anderson, who at sixty-eight is a retired postal worker living off a small social security pension in rural Minnesota. Every month, when his check comes in, he contributes part of it to his local Childbirth Education Association; for over a year he contributed regularly to support a lawsuit against a hospital in Louisiana which refused to allow fathers into the delivery room. Why? When he was a young man, he was not allowed to attend at the birth of his own children, and he feels, to this day, that he missed one of the most exciting and important experiences of a lifetime.

Despite the reluctance of many hospitals to recognize the feelings of men about childbirth, the prognosis for more father involvement in the delivery room is hopeful. For as the birth rate declines, hospitals are competing for the maternity business. They are being forced to respond more to the demands of their consumers; and more of their consumers are men who are finding support—as Earl Anderson could not some forty years ago—from the childbirth education movement.

170

Promotion of fathers' inclusion in the delivery of their children is an important step in allowing men to feel right from the beginning that taking care of children is not just a "women's issue."

CREATING A DIALOGUE ABOUT FATHERHOOD

If a woman in our society wants to examine—or share her feelings about—her role as a mother, she can usually engage in a dialogue, if not with her husband, then most probably with her female neighbors, or friends, or perhaps with her women's group. Men find such occasions for dialogue harder to come by.

Consider Roger Wilson, age thirty-three, father of two, the parts manager for a Chevrolet dealer in New York City. Without admitting to himself that he wanted a setting where he could—through discussion with other men—gain some perspective on his role as a father, he signed up for a course listed as "Parenthood" by the adult education division of the local high school. When he arrived for the first class meeting, he found himself the only man among thirty-four women. And from the syllabus of the course, it was clear that "parenthood" meant "motherhood." He sat through the first class, uncomfortably, and never returned.

Most courses in parenthood are not much more supportive of male involvement. According to Dr. Joyce Sullivan, head of the Home Economics Department at the University of Akron, they are "discussions of lactation and pregnancy." Dr. Sullivan did something to change that when, in 1973, she began offering her course entitled "Fatherhood," the first of its kind ever offered at a college or university in the United States.

Since its inception, "Fatherhood," listed in the university catalog under Home Economics and Family Ecology, has enrolled some two hundred men and women of varying parental status: the thirty-two-year-old father of three who works in the Goodyear plant, an eighteen-year-old girl who felt she never really knew her father, a twenty-six-year-old police officer who was expecting his first child, a disabled Vietnam veteran who found himself with lots of time at home. The course relies heavily on discussion with guests: single adoptive fathers, men who have "coached" the birth of their children, attorneys specializing in family law, and so forth. Enrollment has increased every year as men and women discover there is a local forum for discussion of the role of men in child rearing. For many students, the course legitimizes as a scholarly pursuit the exploration of a subject that affects their personal lives very directly. And for a few, it has been a real eye-opener; men who had no idea they could be present at the birth of their children have, after listening to David and Linda Bailey, copresidents of Akron's Childbirth Education Association, become ardent proponents of husband-coached childbirth.

Originally offered on a once-a-year basis, "Fatherhood" has become so popular that it is now offered every academic quarter. Over 250 colleges and universities scattered in forty states have asked for information so that they can implement similar courses, and Dr. Sullivan is planning to publish a national newsletter on fatherhood. But it is not just where academic credit is available that interest is jelling. Bob Smith, an electrical engineer from Rhode Island, organized a group in his local church—men ranging in age from twenty-three to fifty-five—who wanted to begin exploring their roles as fathers. And in Boston, Massachusetts, an organization called C.O.P.E. (Coping with the Overall Pregnancy Experience), founded initially to provide postpartum support to mothers, is planning to extend its support to fathers as well.

Ideally, courses in parenthood would address the common needs and experiences of parents, be they mothers or fathers. As we work towards that ideal, as we work to overcome the notion that "parent" equals "mother," special courses and support groups for fathers should be encouraged at colleges, universities, continuing education programs, hospitals, and so on. For there are, indeed, more men like Roger Wilson who are looking for a place to begin examining their role in the child-rearing process.

REWRITING THE CHILD-REARING MANUALS

If the number of child-care manuals published each year is any indication, there is no limit to the concern American parents have about *how to* take care of their children. John DeFrain, a sociologist by profession and a collector of child-care manuals by hobby, found that in 1973 there were at least fifty-three current guidebooks to which he could turn for advice.

> From the books on my shelf, I can cull literally hundreds of discussions of bedwetting, spanking, breast feeding, whining, discipline, babysitters, impetigo, pin worms, and the like. If you want to know how to talk "childrenese," how to play with your child, how to communicate with your child, or how to give your child a superior mind, I can refer you to the proper texts. . . . And, if you wish to hear of "the awesome responsibility of parenthood," I can show you chapters and verses.

The only issue ignored by almost all child-care manuals, found DeFrain, was "one of the most important issues that confronts parents today—*who* shall bear the direct responsibility for raising children." [12]

In *Baby and Child Care,* to cite the largest selling child-care manual of all time, Dr. Spock advised fathers to change an occasional diaper; but he cautioned about trying to force the participation of "fathers who get gooseflesh at the very idea of helping to take care of a baby." [13]

There are, however, signs of change. The eminent pediatrician has apologized publicly for the sexism implicit in his popular manual. And in 1974, as he set about revising *Baby and Child Care* to reflect his new views, his new book, *Raising Children in a Difficult Time,* had this to say:

> The father—any father—should be sharing with the mother the day-to-day care of their child from birth onward, I believe. This is the natural (unforced) way for the father to start the relationship, just as it is for the mother. . . . I feel that a father during the hours when he is at home, in the morning, in the evening, and on weekends, should put in as much time as the mother on child care, whether or not the mother has an outside job too. She is either tired as a result of her job or she is tired of taking care of the children. [14]

Meanwhile, local bookstores have begun displaying titles addressed specifically to men: *How to Father* by Fitzhugh Dodson, *Bachelor Fatherhood* by Michael McFadden, *What's a*

Father For? by Sara Gilbert, and *Father Power* by Dr. Henry Biller and Dennis Meredith.

The new books about fatherhood are responding to and, in part, helping to stimulate an increasing attention in our society to the role of men in child rearing. Like special courses in fatherhood, they represent a trend towards a more balanced perspective and provide one more source of encouragement to men who want to examine the effects on themselves of cultural norms about men and children. There is *wide* variation, however, in the guidance offered by the new manuals. In some cases, they go one step forward and at least two steps back.

For example, Fitzhugh Dodson's *How to Father*, introduced in 1974 as "the first [book] written specifically for the child-rearing father," never assumes for a minute that fathers can or should have anything but an adjunct role in child care. "Few things are more rewarding emotionally than the delight a man gets from satisfactorily guiding his children from birth through their various stages of development," asserts Dr. Dodson.[15] But in his world, fathers go off to work in the morning leaving mothers—none of whom have jobs of their own—to reap both the emotional rewards and the difficulties of a day with the kids. Nor does it cross Dodson's mind that, in the event of divorce, a man might *seek* custody of his children. "I know of a mother with a severe alcoholic problem who was wise enough to let the father have custody." [16]

The most significant book to date about men and child rearing is *Father Power* by psychologist Henry Biller and journalist Dennis Meredith. Theirs is not a guide for changing diapers, but for understanding—and changing—our society's script about father-child relations. They range from the choice of an obstetrician—"[it] should be a joint decision, with each of you contributing on the basis of your own observations. . . . If the doctor does not recognize you as a viable member of the husband-wife team, look elsewhere"—to the choice of a day-care center.

> Both of you should be involved in looking for day care for the baby. Make sure you visit the setting and talk to other par-

ents who have children before making a decision. Try to find a setting close to where one or both of you work so you can visit during your work day. . . . Neither you nor your wife should be reticent about presenting your special needs to your employer; you should explain to her or him that you may need special time off or will want to work unconventional hours or even bring the child to work with you occasionally. Most essential, realize that your fatherhood is as important as your career.[17]

Simplistic? Unrealistic? Visionary? Biller and Meredith are merely saying aloud and to men what women think to themselves silently before making decisions about work. And they are touching on *the* issue central to any discussion of child rearing in the future, for the serious encouragement of men to child-caring responsibility means questioning our existing economic structure and the competitive, individualistic, achievement-oriented ethic that underlies it. It means placing our value primarily on the family, saying that it is society's job not just to create conditions in which individuals achieve and produce, but in which the internal, stable functioning of the family is promoted.

THE COMPLEXITY AND BENEFITS OF CHANGE

To think that books on child rearing or children's books or courses for fathers will produce some radical change in our society would be naive. And yet, it would be equally naive to ignore the enormous social benefits that would result from any mechanism that helped to break down those barriers that constrict the role of men in child rearing.

If men are encouraged from childhood through adolescence and adulthood to feel that their own sense of personal identity can be built on direct caring, and not just on providing, they will feel less of a need to invest everything in breadwinning and career. How many men feel worthless as fathers without their monthly paycheck? For how many men is self-esteem proportional to the size of the paycheck? This is not to say that men shouldn't be providers or take pride in their success. But a broadened sense of manhood will relieve men of some of the burdens attached to providing, and will allow some to experience more fully the achievement of helping their children grow. There may be new anxieties—some of the anxieties women now have about whether or not they are good enough mothers. But these anxieties will, if expressed, be healthy, for they will increase the communication between men and women, let them share more fully in the experience of their parenthood.

Just as the pressures will be off men to pin their identity on success outside the home, the pressures on women to pin their identities on motherhood will be reduced. Growing up in a world where they know that men can and want to take care of young children, women will not feel so guilty if they find that, though they want to bear children, they don't want to care for them all the time. Already surveys show that marriages in which husbands and wives share all areas of responsibility tend to be the happiest. In marriages where child care is shared, there will be less chance for the development within individual households of what Dr. Jessie Bernard calls "the two marriages —his and hers." [18] Furthermore, greater social acceptability of the male child rearer will, when marriages end in divorce, relieve many women of the feeling that they *have* to seek custody.

Children will benefit too. The sharing of child rearing between men and women will reduce the isolation of contemporary motherhood and many of its consequent emotional stresses. And in those families in which men stay home full time as househusbands, the quality of child care may even improve, because a factor essential to the high quality of such care is the care giver's choice of the role. With the breakdown of stereotypes about what it means to be a man, we may support the choices of those men especially interested in and capable of caring for their young children.

But it is not only within the family that children will receive better care. As men become more involved with the care of young children, they will realize what millions of American women have known all along: that there are limits to the human ability to offer nurturant response, that the care of young children is an exciting but also an enervating activity,

176

that parents are often best able to give to their children if they can share in their giving. And in a society where the extended family no longer exists, that means advocating—and adding more political clout for—the development of high-quality day-care programs to serve the children of both "working mothers" and "working fathers." (An example of this was given on October 8, 1975, when Senate Finance Chairman Russell Long, traditionally an opponent of strict federal staffing requirements for child-care centers, proposed a bill to give states additional money to help them upgrade staff-child ratios in day care. "I didn't know how much work was involved in caring for kids until my daughter had a baby," said Long to members of Congress who opposed his bill. "If you look after those children—three and four year olds—for a few days, you will want to come back to the U.S. Senate and do your legislative chores.") [19]

How likely are we to see a "new fatherhood"? No culture changes its patterns of child rearing quickly. As the lives of men who have chosen primary child-caring roles suggest, these patterns are tied to every aspect of social and economic organization, to legal traditions, and to widely held beliefs about what is "naturally" appropriate for men and women. But consider this: Ten years ago, there were *no* single adoptive fathers; househusbands were unheard of; even fewer men were seeking custody of their children; and there were *no* colleges or businesses willing to let male professionals work part time so they could be involved in child care. And ten years ago, nobody would have predicted these results from a 1974 Roper survey of a representative sample of American men: "When asked what would be the most satisfying and interesting way of life, almost half of all men (44 percent) say 'a marriage where husband and wife share responsibilities more—both work, both share homemaking and child responsibilities." [20]

The prospect of a society freed from stereotypes about child caring is both liberating and, in many ways, threatening. After all, the constriction of possibilities makes life simpler for men and women as they grow up; at least they know what lies ahead, what to prepare for. There is security for men and women in knowing that fathers are, first and foremost, bread-winners, and that mothers—even mothers with full-time jobs outside the home—take care of the children. But the personal costs of our stereotypes become more apparent every day.

It seems to me that men and women are looking for ways to make their individual lives and their families work. All too often, change seems impossible. The rules that say men and women should lead very different lives, especially when it comes to child rearing, come from without and they come from within. The structure of work, attitudes bred into us, all seem to militate against change. And yet, it seems that when people get even the slightest bit of evidence that change is possible, when their feelings and desires are confirmed, they are em-powered to try to change themselves. And so, finally, looking to the future, I offer this book as one other bit of confirming evi-dence—hoping that even a few lives, when shared, will help create new possibilities for us all.

NOTES

1. At hearings of the Senate Subcommittee on Children and Youth on the Child and Family Services Act of 1975 (S.626), Senator James Buckley of New York and child psychologist Dr. Rhoda Lorand, among others, argued against the bill's support of day-care services. According to Dr. Lorand, "Young children develop best when in the care of their mothers (assuming the mother is reasonably normal) and . . . the emotional sustenance provided by the mother's loving care and interest are indispensable to cognitive growth. . . . It is therefore a great mistake to encourage women to leave their preschoolers in institutional day-care and take employment."

2. Dr. Urie Bronfenbrenner, "Public Policy and the Survival of Families," *Voice for Children* 8, no. 4 (April 1975), p. 2. Emphasis added.

3. Jean Hallaire, *Part-time Employment: Its Extent and Problems* (Paris: Organization for Economic Cooperation and Development, 1968), p. 99.

4. Marc Feigen Fasteau, *The Male Machine* (New York: Mc-Graw-Hill, 1975), p. 98.

5. Shulamith Firestone, *The Dialectic of Sex: The Case for Feminist Revolution* (New York: Bantam Books, 1971), p. 72.

CHAPTER 1   MOTHERS, FATHERS, AND EXPERTS

1. Leon Friedman, " 'Fathers Don't Make Good Mothers,' Said the Judge," *New York Times*, Sunday, January 28, 1973, Section IV, p. 12.

2. Bennett Olshaker, M.D., *What Shall We Tell the Kids?* (New York: Arbor House, 1971), p. 27.

3. Dr. Haim Ginott, *Between Parent and Child* (New York: Macmillan, 1975), pp. 168–169.

4. Bruno Bettelheim, Ph.D., "Fathers Shouldn't Try to Be Mothers," *Parents' Magazine* (October 1956), pp. 124–125.

5. Sigmund Freud, *An Outline of Psychoanalysis* (New York: W. W. Norton, 1940, 1949), p. 45.

6. John Bowlby, *Maternal Care and Mental Health* (1951, *Bulletin of the World Health Organization* 3; reprint edition, New York: Schocken Books, 1966, p. 15; or in John Bowlby, *Child Care and the Growth of Love*, Penguin Books, 1965, p. 21).

7. *Ibid.*, p. 13 and p. 15.

8. Margaret Mead, "Some Theoretical Considerations on the Problem of Mother-Child Separation," *American Journal of Orthopsychiatry* 24, No. 3 (1964), p. 480.

9. Leonard Benson, *Fatherhood: A Sociological Perspective* (New York: Random House, 1968), p. 272.

10. Angela Barron MacBride, *The Growth and Development of Mothers* (New York: Harper and Row, 1973), p. 11.

11. Eleanor Emmons Maccoby and Carol Nagy Jacklin, *The Psychology of Sex Differences* (Palo Alto: Stanford University Press, 1975), p. 216.

12. Michael E. Lamb, ed., *The Role of the Father in Child Development* (New York: Wiley, scheduled publication August 1976), p. 94.

13. Rochelle Paul Wortis, "The Acceptance of the Concept of the Maternal Role by Behavioral Scientists: Its Effects on Women," *American Journal of Orthopsychiatry* 41, No. 5 (1971), p. 738.

14. Mary C. Howell, "Effects of Marital Employment on the Child (II)," *Pediatrics* 52, No. 3 (September 1973), p. 14.

15. Mary C. Howell, "Employed Mothers and Their Families," *Pediatrics* 52, No. 2 (August 1973), p. 7.

16. Daniel R. Miller and Guy E. Swanson, *The Changing American Parent* (New York: Wiley, 1958); Robert R. Sears, Eleanor E. Maccoby, and Harry Levin, *Patterns of Child Rearing* (Evanston, Ill.: Row, Peterson, 1957); Robert O. Blood and Donald M. Wolfe, *Husbands and Wives: The Dynamics of Married Living* (New York: Free Press, 1960); William Goode, *After Divorce* (New York: Free Press, 1956).

17. Frank A. Pedersen, Ph.D., and Kenneth S. Robson, M.D., "Father Participation in Infancy," *American Journal of Orthopsychiatry* 39, No. 3 (April 1969), pp. 467–468.

18. These and other examples of neglect of the father's role are elaborated in E. E. LeMasters, *Parents in Modern America*, revised edition (Homewood, Ill.: Dorsey Press, 1974), p. 125.

19. Henry B. Biller, *Father, Child, and Sex Role* (Lexington, Mass.: D. C. Heath, 1971), p. 18.

20. There is a growing critique, long overdue, of the prejudice and limitations built into any psychological tests that rely on the cultural constructs "masculinity" and "femininity." Clinical psychologist James Harrison has written a brilliant historical analysis of the development and maintenance of "masculinity" and "femininity" as norms in psychological testing in "A Critical Evaluation of Research on 'Masculinity/Femininity' and A Proposal for an Alternative Paradigm for Research on Psychological Differences and Similarities Between the Sexes" (Ph.D. dissertation, New York University, October 1974). Stanford psychologist Dr. Sandra Lipsitz Bem has developed the first test that does not make traits associated with traditionally "masculine" or "feminine" sex roles mutually exclusive. The Bem Sex-Role Inventory, which measures "psychological androgyny," indicates that the more people combine traits stereotypically thought appropriate only to men or to women, the more flexible—and healthy—they are, the more able to respond with situationally appropriate behavior. See, among Dr. Bem's many publications, "The Measurement of Psychological Androgyny," *Journal of Consulting and Clinical Psychology* 42, No. 2 (1974), pp. 155–162; or "Androgyny vs. the Tight Little Lives of Fluffy Women and Chesty Men," *Psychology Today* 9, No. 4 (September 1975), pp. 58–62.

21. Ross D. Parke and Sandra O'Leary, "Father-Mother-Infant Interaction in the Newborn Period: Some Findings, Some Observations, and Some Unresolved Issues," in K. Riegel and J. Meachem, eds., *The Developing Individual in a Changing*

World Vol. II, *Social and Environmental Issues* (The Hague: Morton, 1975).

22. Martin Greenberg, M.D., and Norman Morris, M.D., "Engrossment: The Newborn's Impact Upon the Father," *American Journal of Orthopsychiatry* 44, No. 4 (July 1974), pp. 522, 523 528.

23. *Ibid.*, p. 527.

24. For a thorough review of the literature, see Robert A. Fein, "Men's Experiences Before and After the Birth of a First Child: Dependence, Marital Sharing, and Anxiety" (Ph.D. dissertation, Harvard University, 1974); and John Henry Wapner, "An Empirical Approach to the Attitudes, Feelings and Behaviors of Expectant Fathers" (Ph.D. dissertation, Northwestern University, 1975).

25. R. H. Munroe, "Pregnancy Symptoms Among Expectant American Fathers: An Inquiry Into the Psychological Meaning" (Ed.D. dissertation, Harvard University, 1964).

26. Robert A. Fein, *op. cit.* (note 24), pp. 17–18.

27. Milton Kotelchuck, "The Nature of the Child's Tie to His Father" (Ph.D. dissertation, Harvard University, April 1972), p. 141.

28. *Ibid.*, p. 143. Findings of Kotelchuck and his research colleagues can be found in more condensed form in Kotelchuck, Zelazo, Kagan, and Spelke, "Infant Reaction to Parental Separations When Left with Familiar and Unfamiliar Adults," *Journal of Genetic Psychology* 126 (1975), pp. 255–262; Ross, Kagan, Zelazo, and Kotelchuck, "Separation Protest in Infants in Home and Laboratory," *Developmental Psychology* 11 (1975), pp. 256–257; and Spelke, Zelazo, Kagan, and Kotelchuck, "Father Interaction and Separation Protest," *Developmental Psychology* 9 (1973), pp. 83–90. Research with similar findings has been reported by L. J. Cohen and J. J. Campos, "Father, Mother, and Stranger as Elicitors of Attachment Behaviors in Infancy," *Developmental Psychology* 10 (1974), pp. 146–154, and in an increasing number of papers from a longitudinal study conducted by Michael Lamb while at Yale University (he has recently moved to University of Wisconsin-Madison): "Infant Attachment to Mothers and Fathers" (paper presented to the Society for Research in Child Development, Denver, April 1975); "Infants, Fathers, and Mothers: Interaction at Eight Months of Age in the Home and in the Laboratory" (paper presented to the Eastern Psychological Association, New York, April 1975);

"Interactions between Two-Year-Olds and Their Mothers and Fathers" (unpublished manuscript, Yale University, 1975); "Twelve-Month-Olds and Their Parents: Interaction in a Laboratory Playroom" (unpublished manuscript, Yale University, 1975); "Proximity Seeking Attachment Behaviors: A Critical Review of the Literature," *Genetic Psychology Monographs,* 1976.

29. William K. Redican and Gary Mitchell, "Play Between Adult Male and Infant Rhesus Monkeys," *American Zoology* 14 (1974), p. 296.

30. Gary Mitchell, William K. Redican, and Jody Gomber, "Lesson from a Primate: Males Can Raise Babies," *Psychology Today* (April 1974), p. 67.

31. *Ibid.,* p. 68.

CHAPTER 2   CONFRONTING FATHERHOOD: MEN AND CUSTODY

1. James P. Rorris, "Separation Agreements—Support for the Spouse and Minor Children," *Minnesota Family Law, Minnesota Practice Manual 50* (Minneapolis: University of Minnesota, 1971), p. 75.

2. Henry Foster, Jr., and Doris Jonas Freed, *Law and the Family —New York* (Rochester, N.Y.: The Lawyers Co-Operative Publishing Co., 1968, 1972), Vol. 2, p. 512.

3. Massachusetts General Laws, Chapter 298, Paragraph 31.

4. Utah Code Annotated, Section 30–3–10.

5. All information and citations from Melvin L. Wulf and Rena K. Uviller, "Petition for a Writ of Certiorari to the Supreme Court of Utah," David Arends, Petitioner, against Edwina Arends, Respondent, in the Supreme Court of the United States, October Term, 1973.

6. "Opinion of the Supreme Court of the State of Utah," No. 13349, filed January 2, 1974. A copy of this opinion appears in an appendix to the ACLU petition on behalf of David Arends.

7. King v. DeManneville, 5 East 221, 102 Eng. Rep. 1054 (K.B. 1804) in Morris Ploscowe and Doris Jonas Freed, *Family Law: Cases and Materials* (Boston: Little, Brown, 1963), p. 469.

8. Robert C. Brown, "The Custody of Children," *Indiana Law Journal* 2 (1926–27), p. 326; Jenkins v. Jenkins, 173 Wis. 592, 181 N.W. 826, 827, 1921; cited in State Ex Rel Watts v. Watts, 350 N.Y.S. 2nd 285, p. 289.

9. Chapsky v. Wood, 26 Kan. 650, 40 Am. Rep. 321 (1881), in

Morris Ploscowe and Doris Jonas Freed, *op. cit.* (note 7), p. 471.

10. Bradwell v. Illinois, 83 U.S. 130, 141 (1872), cited in Lila Tritico, "Child Custody: Preference to the Mother," *Louisiana Law Review* 34 (Summer 1974), p. 883.

11. Andrew S. Watson, M.D., "The Children of Armageddon: Problems of Custody Following Divorce," *Syracuse Law Review* 21 (1969–1970), p. 67.

12. *Ibid.*, p. 70.

13. Robert J. Levy and Phoebe C. Ellsworth, "Legislative Reform of Child Custody Adjudication," *Law and Society Review* 4 (November 1969), p. 168.

14. *Ibid.*, p. 198.

15. *Ibid.*, p. 202.

16. *Ibid.*, pp. 202–203. Emphasis added.

17. Kelin E. Gersick, "Psychological and Situational Determinants in Fathers' Decisions Whether or Not to Seek Custody of Their Children in Divorce Proceedings" (unpublished prospectus of Psychology and Social Relations, Harvard University, May 24, 1974), p. 5.

18. Minner v. Minner, Equity case n. 43045, Circuit Court of Montgomery County, Maryland, January 22, 1973; cited in *Washington Post*, August 12, 1974, p. A-3.

19. Fla. Stat. 61.13 (2), F.S.A. (1971).

20. Moezie v. Moezie, Civil Action No. D 3535–71, Superior Court of the District of Columbia, Family Division, January 19, 1973.

21. State ex rel Watts v. Watts, 350 N.Y.S. 2d 285, p. 289.

22. Robert J. Levy and Phoebe C. Ellsworth, *op. cit.* (note 13), p. 219.

23. Missouri is the only state that keeps a record of custody disposition. Figures from the Missouri Center for Health Statistics indicate a declining percentage of custody awards made to men: In 1960, 11,253 divorces resulted in 458 (7.9 percent) custody awards to fathers; in 1968, 16,389 divorces resulted in 714 (7.6 percent) custody awards to fathers; in 1973, the latest year for which figures are available, 21,670 divorces resulted in 776 custody awards to fathers, a drop to 6.4 percent ("Reported Divorces and Annulments by Number of Children Affected," Missouri Center for Health Statistics, Jefferson, Mo.).

24. Dr. Paul Glick, "Children Living With a Currently Divorced Parent, by Sex of Parent and Age of Child, for The United

States: 1974, 1970, 1960," unpublished chart compiled from U.S. Bureau of the Census, *Current Population Reports,* Series P-20, No. 271, "Marital Status and Living Arrangements: March 1974"; *1970 Census of Population,* Vol. II, 4B, *Persons by Family Characteristics,* table 1; and 1960 Census of Population, Vol. I, *U.S. Summary,* table 185.

25. Bernard Schlesinger, *One-Parent Family* (Toronto: University of Toronto Press, 1969).
26. Painter v. Bannister, Iowa: 1392 N.W. 153, cited in Robert J. Levy and Phoebe C. Ellsworth, *op. cit.* (note 13), p. 168.
27. Joseph Goldstein, Anna Freud, and Albert J. Solnit, *Beyond the Best Interests of the Child* (New York: The Free Press, 1973), pp. 62–63.
28. *Ibid.,* p. 62.
29. *Ibid.,* p. 63.
30. *Ibid.,* p. 32.
31. *Ibid.,* p. 153.
32. Susan Gettleman and Janet Markowitz, *The Courage to Divorce* (New York: Simon and Schuster, 1974), pp. 217, 219.
33. Henry Biller, Ph.D., and Dennis Meredith, *Father Power* (New York: David McKay, 1974), p. 281.
34. For information, contact Ms. Diana Dubroff, N.O.I.S.E. Abused Children of America, Inc., 12 W. 72 St., New York, N.Y. 10023.
35. New Jersey legislation reported in *New York Times,* February 16, 1974, p. 26; October 1, 1974, p. 87.
36. Henry Foster and Doris Jonas Freed, "A Bill of Rights for Children," *New York Law Journal,* July 28, 1972, August 25, 1972, and September 22, 1972; "Shuffled Child and Divorce Court," *Trial* 10 (May–June 1974), p. 26.
37. Carolyn Shaw Bell, "Alternatives for Social Change: The Future Status of Women" (unpublished paper presented at the Mr. and Mrs. Spencer T. Olin Conference on The Status of Women in Higher Education and the Professions, at Washington University, St. Louis, Missouri, April 16–17, 1975), p. 18.
38. *Ibid.,* p. 19.
39. Michael Wheeler, *No-Fault Divorce* (Boston: Beacon Press, 1974), p. 97.
40. California Civil Code Section 4600 (West 1970), as amended ch. 1007, Section 1 (1972) Cal. Stats. 1855; cited in Henry Foster and Doris Jonas Freed, "Divorce Reform: Brakes on Breakdown?" *Journal of Family Law* 13 (1973–74), p. 485.

CHAPTER 3 MAKING THE TIME TO CARE: PART-TIME JOBS
FOR FULL-TIME FATHERS

1. *The Wall Street Journal,* September 24, 1974, p. 24.
2. 1970 Census of the Population, cited in Carolyn Shaw Bell, "Full Employment: Implications for Women," *Social Policy* 3, no. 3 (September-October 1972), p. 14.
3. Jerome Rosow, ed., *The Changing World of Work* (Englewood Cliffs, N.J.: Prentice-Hall, 1974), p. x; the advantages to business and family life of flexible hours are presented in a survey conducted by Virginia Martin and edited by Jo Hartley of the Business and Professional Women's Foundation: "Hours of Work When Workers Can Choose: The Experience of 59 Organizations with Employee-chosen Staggered Hours and Flexitime," available for $2.00 from BPW Foundation, 2012 Massachusetts Avenue, N.W., Washington, D.C. 20036.
4. Mark Goldsmith, "Part-Time Jobs Liberate Both Parents," *Christian Science Monitor,* October 9, 1974, p. 10; further analysis of the experiment appears in papers by Erik Gronseth: "Work-Sharing Families: Husband and Wife Both in Part-time Employment" (paper presented at conference, "Partnership Tomorrow," at the Gottlieb Duttweiler Institute, Ruschlikon by Zurich, June 1972); "Notes Towards a Scientific Framework for Life-Affirmative Family Policies" (paper presented ICOFA seminar, Dubrovnik, December 1972).
5. Advisory Council to the Prime Minister on Equality Between Men and Women in Sweden, working paper, 1974.
6. Letter from Roxanne Barton Conlin to Ms. Susan Schwerin, December 10, 1973.
7. Carol S. Greenwald, "Working Mothers: The Need for More Part-time Jobs," *New England Economic Review* (September/October 1972), p. 21.
8. *Ibid.,* p. 21.
9. [Mary O'Meara], *Part-time Social Workers in Public Welfare: A Report on a Catalyst Demonstration Project in Boston, Massachusetts, in Which Mature Women College Graduates Were Employed Half-time by the Massachusetts Department of Public Welfare* (New York: Catalyst, October 1971).
10. Marjorie M. Silverberg and Lorraine D. Eyde, "Career Part-time Employment: Personnel Implications of the HEW Professional and Executive Corps," *Good Government* (Fall 1971), pp. 11–20.

11. Carol Greenwald, "Working Mothers," *op. cit.* (note 7), p. 19; also Gloria Dapper and Judith Murphy, *Part-time Teachers and How They Work: A Study of Five School Systems"* (New York: Catalyst, December 1968).

12. [Gretl Meier, Barbara Marmer, Barney Olmstead, and Linda Schuck], *Job Sharing in the Schools: A Study of Nine Bay Area Districts* (Palo Alto: New Ways to Work, February 1976).

13. Cheryl A. Stewart, Jeanne L. Kennedy, Christine M. Sierra, and Charles W. Gossett, *Job Sharing in Municipal Government: A Case Study in the City of Palo Alto* (Stanford, Calif.: Stanford University Action Research Liaison Office, June 1975).

14. Nadine Brozan, "Part-Time Workers—Making Inroads into a Full-Time World," *New York Times* (October 16, 1973), p. 38.

15. Introduction to the Senate. of S. 2022, *Congressional Record* 119, No. 95 (June 19, 1973).

16. Studs Terkel, *Working* (New York: Pantheon, 1972), pp. xxxiii–xxxiv.

CHAPTER 4   ULTRAPLANNED PARENTHOOD: SINGLE ADOPTIVE FATHERS

1. Joseph Epstein, *Divorced in America: Marriage in an Age of Possibility* (New York: Penguin Books, 1975), p. 178.

2. Benjamin Schlesinger's *The One-Parent Family: Perspectives and Annotated Bibliography* (Canada: University of Toronto Press, 1969) reveals the extent to which students of the single-parent family have presumed it to be pathological.

3. Velma L. Jordan and William F. Little, "Early Comments on Single-Parent Adoptive Homes," *Child Welfare* (November 1966), pp. 536–538.

4. Statistics provided in letter from Lenore K. Campbell, Director, Department of Adoptions, Los Angeles County, April 24, 1975.

5. "Should a Single Person Adopt a Child?" *Good Housekeeping*, August 1969, p. 16.

6. Bernice Q. Madison, "Adoption: Yesterday, Today, and Tomorrow—Part II," *Child Welfare* (June 1966), p. 347.

7. "Test Allows Single Women to Adopt," *New York Times*, Friday, May 12, 1967, p. 23.

8. Letter from Audrey V. Yarbrough, Supervisor of Adoption Services, Tennessee Department of Public Welfare, Nashville, Tenn., in "Reader's Exchange," *Children* 17, No. 4 (July–August 1970), p. 163.

9. One instance where the record did become available for pub-

lic examination is reported in Scott Moore, "In One Household: James Bond and Bachelor Father," *San Jose Mercury* (April 15, 1968), p. 33. According to the article, "On March 28, 1968, Charles Bond, a 29 year old bachelor and Philco-Ford engineer, become the first single man in the nation ever to adopt a baby. The independent adoption of 7 month old James was finalized by Santa Clara Superior Court Judge Paul T. Gallagher over the strenuous objections of the Welfare Department. Bond had brought James home from the hospital when he was four days old, and began rearing him in his modern three bedroom home in Lakewood Village which he rents. The home is roomy, comfortable, surrounded by lush landscaping, and located in a well-kept neighborhood of young marrieds. The objection presented by the social welfare department was that the home wasn't suitable. In making his decision to grant the adoption, Judge Gallagher had a report on Charles Bond from Dr. Leo R. Ryan, chief psychologist at Agnews State Hospital, who tested and interviewed Bond and concluded: 'According to the tests, most people would see Bond as a reasonably social individual who tends not to interfere with others, a person who is cautious about getting emotionally involved with others. That is, he should be perceived as somewhat reserved. Characteristically, he is more of a homebody rather than a party-goer. Bond also is quite independent in his thinking. Not only is he an independent thinker, but also he is quite bright. It appears from the testing results that Bond is well prepared for the rigors of raising a child, especially a boy. He does not react with excitability or ineffectiveness when confronted with stress. . . . Bond not only has the proper temperament and motivation for raising a boy, but also is financially capable, gainfully employed, and lives in an ample sized house located in a socially acceptable environment for raising children. . . . there are strong indications that he is capable of providing quite adequate psychological and social management of the child's welfare.' "

CHAPTER 5   THE OTHER WAY ROUND: HOUSEHUSBANDS

1. U.S. Department of Labor, *Dictionary of Occupational Titles*, 3rd ed., Vol. 1, Definitions of Titles; Vol. 2, Occupational Classifications (Washington, D.C.: U.S Government Printing Office, 1965); for an analysis of the D.O.T. rating system, see Briggs, "Guess Who Has the Most Complex Job?" in Babcock, Freedman, Norton, and Ross, *Sex Discrimination and the Law:*

Causes and Remedies (Boston: Little, Brown, 1975), pp. 203–205; also available from Briggs, Division of Apprenticeship and Training, 310 Price Place, Madison, Wis. 53701.

2. Norman W. Bell and Ezra Vogel, eds., *A Modern Introduction to the Family*, revised edition (New York: Free Press, 1968), p. 32.

3. This characterization of housewife syndrome, as well as a lucid review of sociological and psychological research on housewives, can be found in Jessie Bernard, *The Future of Marriage* (New York: Bantam Books, 1973), p. 32.

4. Rhona and Robert Rapoport, *Dual-Career Families* (Baltimore, Maryland: Penguin Books, 1971), p. 8.

5. *Ibid.*

6. According to economist Carolyn Shaw Bell, Bob Johnson's reference to "other women" is the type of slip of the tongue made by women working in predominantly male occupations. Dr. Bell reports that she and her female colleagues sometimes find themselves referring to "the other men at the meeting."

7. Jessie Bernard, *op. cit.* (note 3), p. 46.

8. March 1974 figures from the Bureau of Labor Statistics in Employment and Earnings provided in a letter from Carmen R. Maymi, Director, Women's Bureau, Department of Labor, March 24, 1975; October 1975 figures from U.S. Department of Labor, Bureau of Labor Statistics in *Employment and Earnings* 22, No. 4 (October 1975), p. 64.

9. Carolyn Shaw Bell, "Alternatives for Social Change: The Future Status of Women" (unpublished paper presented at the Mr. and Mrs. Spencer T. Olin Conference on The Status of Women in Higher Education and the Professions, at Washington University, St. Louis, Missouri, April 16–17, 1975), p. 12.

10. *Ibid.*, pp. 23–34.

11. The matter of payment was discussed in 1898 by Charlotte Perkins Gilman in *Women and Economics* (Harper Torchbook edition published in 1966). Payment from the employed spouse to the housespouse is discussed by A. C. Scott, "The Value of Housework: For Love or Money?" *Ms. Magazine* (July 1972), pp. 56–58. Government payment has been proposed by many individuals and organizations. See, for example, Jonnie Tillmon, "Welfare Is a Women's Issue," in Klagsburn, ed., *The First Ms. Reader* (1973), or "Report of the Marriage and Family Committee of the National Organization for Women, Suggested Guidelines in Studying and Comments on the Uniform Marriage

and Divorce Act" (1971). For calculations of the value of housework, see, among others: Juanita Kreps, *Sex in the Marketplace: American Women at Work* (Baltimore: The Johns Hopkins Press, 1971); Walker and Gauger, "The Dollar Value of Household Work," Department of Consumer Economics and Public Policy, N.Y. State College of Human Ecology, Cornell University (1973); Stuart M. Speiser, "Recovery from Wrongful Death," in *Economic Handbook* (1970). Excerpts from most of these appear in Babcock, Freedman, Norton, and Ross, *op. cit* (note 1), pp. 658–672. For a thorough analysis of "Mother's Wages" as a social policy alternative, see David G. Gil, *Unraveling Social Policy* (Cambridge, Mass.: Schenkman Publishing Co., 1973).

12. Marianne Millgardh and Berit Rollen, "Parents' Insurance," *Current Sweden,* no. 76 (April 1975), p. 2.

13. Shawn G. Kennedy, "Paternity Leave for Teaching Fathers: An Idea That Has Not Caught Fire," *New York Times,* July 9, 1975, p. 43.

14. *Ibid.*

CHAPTER 6   WHO WILL RAISE THE CHILDREN?

1. Olof Palme, "Lesson from Sweden: The Emancipation of Man," in Louise Kapp Howe, ed., *The Future of the Family* (New York: Touchstone, 1973), pp. 251–252.

2. Richard Weber, "Sex Role Re-Education in Swedish Schools," *Education in Sweden—No. 10* (New York: Swedish Information Service, November 1970), p. 2.

3. Marianne Millgardh and Berit Rollen, "Parents' Insurance," *Current Sweden,* no. 76 (April 1975).

4. Camilla Odhnoff, "Equality Is for Children, Too," *Current Sweden,* No. 98 (March 1976), p. 3.

5. Jessie Bernard, "Prepared Statement of Jessie Bernard, Ph.D., Sociologist," in *American Families: Trends and Pressures, 1973— Hearings Before the Subcommittee on Children and Youth of the Committee on Labor and Public Welfare, September 24, 25, 26, 1973* (Washington, D.C.: U.S. Government Printing Office, 1974).

6. See, for example, *Dick and Jane as Victims: Sex Stereotyping in Children's Readers* by Women on Words and Images (Princeton, N.J.: Women on Words and Images, 1972).

7. Betty Friedan, *The Feminine Mystique* (New York: Dell, 1973), pp. 351, 353.

8. Edward K. Strong, Jr., revised by David P. Campbell, "Manual

for Men's Forms T399 (1966), T399R (1966) and Women's Form W (1946)," *Strong Vocational Interest Blanks* (Stanford: Stanford University Press, 1966).

9. "AMEG Commission Report on Sex Bias in Interest Measurement," *Measurement and Evaluation in Guidance* 6, No. 3 (October 1973), p. 171.

10. David P. Campbell, "Invited Comment: Women Deserve Better," *Personnel and Guidance Journal* 51, No. 8 (April 1973), p. 545.

11. Dr. Frederick Kuder, whose Kuder Occupational Interest Survey is used as widely as the Strong, recommended in 1971, amid the clamor for test revision, that scores for women be reported on both the men's and women's scales of his test, thereby "pointing out to girls occupations or fields of study in which men predominate but opportunities for women are increasing, or for which scales have not yet been developed on women's groups." Kuder did not make the analagous suggestion that men's scores be reported on the women's occupational scales. So, if his suggestions are followed, women automatically get scored on occupations like architect, automobile mechanic, and industrial engineer. However, the only way for a man to be scored as a primary school teacher, nurse, or home economics instructor is to "fool" the test by identifying himself as a woman or by not identifying himself as a man (by leaving the Male-Female blanks unmarked).

12. John D. DeFrain, "A Father's Guide to Parent Guides: Review and Assessment of the Paternal Role as Conceived in the Popular Literature" (paper presented at Annual Meeting of the National Council on Family Relations/American Association of Marriage and Family Counselors, St. Louis, Missouri, October 23–26, 1974), pp. 2–3; available in slightly different form in DeFrain's Ph.D. thesis, *The Nature and Meaning of Parenthood* (University of Wisconsin-Madison, 1975).

13. Dr. Benjamin Spock, *Baby and Child Care* (New York: Pocket Books, 1974), pp. 30–31.

14. Dr. Benjamin Spock, *Raising Children in a Difficult Time* (New York: W. W. Norton, 1974), pp. 242–243. When the revised edition of *Baby and Child Care* appeared in April 1976, Dr. Spock took an even stronger stance (pp. 47–48):

"I think that a father with a full-time job—even where a mother is staying at home—will do best by his children, his wife, and himself if he takes on half or more of the management of the children (and also participates in the housework) when he gets home from work and on weekends. The mother's leadership and patience will probably have worn thin by the end of the day. (The father's would, too, if he alone had had the children all day.) The children will profit from experiencing a variety of styles of leadership and control.

"When a father does his share as a matter of course when at home, it does much more than simply lighten his wife's work load and give her companionship in the work that she has had to do alone all day. It shows that he believes this work is crucial for the welfare of the family, that it calls for judgment and skill and that it's his responsibility as much as it is hers when he is at home. This is what sons and daughters need to see in action if they are to grow up without sexist attitudes.

. . .

"It will be a great day when fathers:

"Consider the care of their children to be as important *to them* as their jobs and careers.

"Seek out jobs and work schedules that will allow them ample time to be with their wives and children.

"Give first consideration, when discussing with their wives where to live, to what favors family life.

"Will resist their companies' attempts to move them frequently.

"Will let it be known at their work places that they take their parental responsibilities very seriously and may have to take time off when their children need them—just as working mothers have always done.

"Will try to get other fathers at their work places to take the same stands."

15. Dr. Fitzhugh Dodson, *How To Father* (Los Angeles: Nash, 1974), p. 4.
16. *Ibid.*, p. 370.
17. Henry Biller, Ph.D., and Dennis Meredith, *Father Power* (New York: David McKay, 1974), pp. 29, 80–81.
18. Jessie Bernard, *The Future of Marriage* (New York: Bantam, 1973).
19. Cited in *Day Care and Child Development Reports*, v. 4, n. 20 (October 13, 1975), p. 2.
20. The Roper Organization, Inc., *The Virginia Slims American Women's Opinion Poll, Volume III* (New York: The Roper Organization and Philip Morris USA, 1974), p. 31.